In *Wildflowers for the Bullies*, Rothenberg takes energetic poetic aim at some of the most glaring political issues of the day, including racism, economic injustice, police brutality, and our overly commercialized culture industry with its "zombie billboards" and "sponsored straightjackets." In his deeply moving poem, "War," Rothenberg uses varied and inventively phrased perspectives ("We imagine the shark a killing machine / We become the killing machine") to note how thoroughly the idea of war has infiltrated Americans' daily lives, offering "love as the answer."

—Eliot Katz, author of *Unlocking the Exits* (Coffee House Press) and *The Poetry and Politics of Allen Ginsberg* (Beatdom Books).

Praise for *Wildflowers for the Bullies*

There is energy in these poems by Michael Rothenberg, fueled by deaths in war, the police killing of 13-year-old Andy Lopez in Santa Rosa, and the deaths of mind and spirit within the malaise of present-day capitalist realities / complexities / obscenities. If truth in ideas and feeling are rare in the official discourse, let these poems ride like galloping horses to break free the truths trapped in the hi-def synthesized madness.

—Luis J. Rodriguez, Poet Laureate of Los Angeles and author of *My Nature is Hunger*

I've often heard "If you're not angry, you're not paying attention." In *Wildflowers for the Bullies* Michael Rothenberg is paying pointed attention to our planet, its people, its ecology, its wars, and in some moments its potential for positive change. He asks necessary and thoughtful questions, "Can poetry make death beautiful?" "Can I hold the wind together?" He is clear that his poetry is not a "poetry with well-articulated parlor room niceness" while declaiming that "We will paint the air black with our voices." In poetry and in prose he bids us to pay attention and be moved to join those who are making change. He also takes us on a thoughtful tour of the USSR, a land of beauty and contradictions and the many people who see and examine what they see in their homeland. In poetry and prose Rothenberg does present the bullies with wildflowers, while making it clear that flowers of every kind will continue to bloom despite the bullies.

—devorah major, San Francisco Poet Laureate Emeritus

Michael Rothenberg has long been a tireless organizer—for poetry and with poetry—to make the world a kinder place. In *Wildflowers for the Bullies*, Rothenberg utters a cri de coeur against the viciousness that is in us and around us, slathered with imperial static. His words pour over the brim of the page, both funny and scary. Rothenberg writes in the key of Ginsberg, if Ginsberg had lived to see Moloch win.

—Philip Metres, activist and author of *Sand Opera* (Alice James, 2015)

It's not often that a collection of poetry grabs and grips the reader like *Wildflowers for the Bullies* by Michael Rothenberg. In it, he bravely and beautifully places squarely before us the ugly realities of the world we live in. His words bring a stark clarity and slow down that world to a crawl from day to agonizing day.

—Jawanza Dumisani, author of *Black Raising Cane Over Red* (Glover Lane Press, 2014).

Wildflowers for the Bullies

Michael Rothenberg

FLOWERSONG
PRESS

FlowerSong Press

Copyright © 2015 by Michael Rothenberg

ISBN: 978-1-953447-46-3

Library of Congress #2022946007

Published by FlowerSong Press

in the United States of America.

www.flowersongpress.com

Cover art by Albert Alvarez. "Justice For All." 2015. Acrylic on panel. 12" x 6." Copyright © 2015 by Albert Alvarez.

Set in Garamond.

Typeset by David A. Romero davidaromero.com

NOTICE: SCHOOLS AND BUSINESSES

FlowerSong Press offers copies of this book at quantity discount with bulk purchase for educational, business, or sales promotional use. For information, please email the publisher at info@flowersongpress.com.

Table of Contents

Wildflowers for the Bullies

Madrigal
(The USSR Journals 1990)

Wildflowers
for the Bullies

War

It can happen any time of the day.
A dislocated anxiety begins in the feet.
Something close to synesthesia,
a red spasm, walks through the clock
towards some vanishing imagination.
A war.

Ameliorate, vilify, shield.
Placate, mollify, hide.
There's nowhere to hide.

Static, static, static. . .

It starts again.
The war.
Topical weariness.
Itchy blades pierce the cheek.
Toxic waves stick to the back of the throat.
A swollen billow, thickening, septic fruit chokes.
Something dirty, dry and tart. . .

The pills I take to cure the tremors don't work anymore.
I don't know that they ever did.

And I'm convinced there never will be
a spirit, powder, plaster, tonic, ointment, filter, malware,
neural concoction that can seize the day
from infectious panic once and for all.
Cure the holocaust.

Untwist the elastic present.
Make love tolerable.

Static, static, end the war, static, love is the answer, static. . .

There never will be a pink calamine,
stainless weed or fermentation,
existential fava or kava
that doesn't have some caustic side effect,
induce some statuary blindness,
dizziness, blurriness, palpitations.
It's an everlasting war.

There never will be a medicine or
moral splint that brings the conflict to an end,
terminates the unceasing war
between consumption and denial.
It's always a war.

There never will be a fizzy pill you can take,
with a tall glass of water,
a splash of lemon, a yoni mantra to align the senses,
ease the pain or repeal the punishment
that flows out of the wreckage.

War,
the universal noun and verb,
moniker for everything we are and do.
Action, inaction, reaction
Re-feathering of the dove.

Static, static, war static.

There's nothing we can do about it.

Static.

War's the word.

Good, bad, and average wars.
Wars against war.

All cheer for war between imaginary gods
and god's sinuous, righteous armies.
Flags of the rich, flags of the poor, crowding the heavens.
Titular banners, combustible standards.
War between the sexes and Twitter personalities.
War between us all!

War,
the unrelenting Dionysian roller coaster,
carnival of megalomaniacal clowns on a Ferris wheel in flames.
Bloodlust bloodbath.
Uncompromising global, local, personal war
waged upon on this planet's rape weary spine.
Everywhere war.
At the toy store, action figures in "the machinery of loss,"
"toy soldiers are our business,"
"taking war to a whole new scale."
On billboards fiery chrome bumpers and monster cylinders
grind out the proto-masculine vendetta
against proto-feminine nature.

War!

Static. Static. Static. . . a symptomatic loop. . .

Do you support the troops?
Kill for cash?
Speculate on The Death Contractors Index?
Military Industrial Complex built into your retirement
pension and health plan, traded like Ebola virus
on the stock exchange.

Where there's money to be made there's no cure or rest.
War is the essential and fundamental currency
of a free enterprise economy.
It's good for me!
I don't care about you!

"A War of Words Apocalypse
pits you up against 3 other players
for an all-out word destruction brawl!"

War against the common cold and sensational rash.
War against poverty.
War against hunger.
War against big gulp obesity and flabby ass.

War against swollen prostate and rectal inadequacies.
War against reluctant and overactive kidneys.
War against lung, lip, tongue, throat, and brain cancer.
War against emotional co-dependency.

Static.

War against sociopathic tendencies.

Static.

War against psychopathic apathies.
War against ambivalence and engagement.
War against silence.
War against speaking out.

Static.

War against drugs and warrior drugs
invented to win the war on drugs.

War against poverty.

Static.

War on the suicidal catwalk between. . . static, static, static. . .
dystopian fashion designers and anorexic supermodels.

War against disbelievers, unbelievers, over and underachievers.

War against aliens from Mexico,
or aliens from anywhere else in outer space.
Star Wars!

War against terrorists, roaches, mice, ants, chinch bugs,
silverfish, moths, lice, bacteria, molds, and poetries.

War against lime deposits in the toilet bowl,
soapy film on the silverware.

Static.

War for the simple thrill of it all.
It's fun to blow things up.
Napalm.
Flame throwers.
Jellied gasoline.
The daily grim game of Reapers in Nevada war rooms.
Drones!
I hear the screams in Pakistan, the collateral damage.
It's all good.
Send a camera into the mysterious and magical
charred wound of a long-distance trophy.
Take a picture, then go home and forget about it all.

Burst into the living room to greet
the loving spouse and happy kiddies
engrossed in more war game videos.
Yay!
Daddy's home.
Mommie's home from war!

War games!
Barrels loaded, bomb bay doors wide open, the rectum release.
The shit of war.
Charge!

Static. Static. Static.

Whoever they are that gets in the way.
Trained assassins and sharpshooter-schoolteachers.

Serial killers and black men in hoodies.
Children on their way to school.
Anyone who stinks up the view of our perfect static world.
Positives and negatives torn to shreds,
liquefied, emulsified, liquidated. . .
Offered for ransom.
You know who you are!

War of the imagination!

Static. Static.

War between vying lovers.
War against creative anxiety crisis and inspiration.
War against maddening crowds and ecclesiastic paradigms.
War against indifference and concern.

The assault of the orgasm.
The soporific split.
War of polar opposites.
Black and white war of shadows.
A colorless war of dichotomies.
The merciless conflagration of yin and yang.
We're here to win and adore the disemboweled challenger.
Show me that trophy again!
End the shame and embarrassment of dreamy pacifists.
Wage more glory!
Wage more war!

Static.

Wage more. . .

Static, war. . .

Tuned to the War Channel history and nature collide,
decide the fate of a hundred extinct civilizations.
The survival of 100 thousand species.
We fill our minds with misanthropic, immortal angels of war.
Mars navigates the ship of death, while Ahab
heralds in the call of the wild.

We imagine the shark a killing machine.
We become the killing machine.

We imagine, in rusty high grass plains
the king of the jungle announces Armageddon.
We become the clarions of destruction.
We roar!
We understand our nature as such.
We know it to be true.
Survival of the fittest is the death of us all!

Everywhere a song of war, fairy tale, lullaby,
whispered in the ear of every child each night
before they go to bed.
A hymn to the species.
Before they go to bed each night they hear this sweet song:

Rock-a-bye baby, before we shoot.
Rock-a-bye baby, a 21-gun salute.

We sing it slow in breathy rounds, rounds and rounds.

Sweet war, sweet, sweet, gentle, war.

We know it to be so.
POW!
We've heard it all before.

I don't know why I feel so tense at night, lying on my back,
un-soothed by the turning fan.

Once more. War. . .

Now I lay me down to sleep, sleep is war, and war is cheap.

Rock-a-bye baby nursery rhymes
waged against daily somnambulism.
Sleep, you little bastard, sleep!

I don't know why I wake up so angry?
A metabolic strychnine creeps through my feet.
I jolt and twitch.

War, war, static, static. . . love is the answer. . .
war static, war static, war.

War between pampered ballet dancers,
amniotic pop singers with sociopathic dreams of stardom.
Beauty queen infants in stiletto heels,
hot red lipstick and a corset of grenades.
Athletes with steel balls.
Gorgeous reality stars with big tits.
Ugly reality stars also with big tits.

Big dicks and big tits flexing a war physique.
Built for war!

War at war with reality.
All at war with fantasy.
At war with joy, employed in war and desperation.
Desperation the high key virtue to war,
the engine and prayer of war.
A table of warring chefs
with knives and peelers flash through flesh.
A stream of *fois gras* and piss.
Drenched in lust while trivia game show contestants
beat the clock to death.
Then finally, the lone gunman
drops into Sandy Hook School one day.
"We will never forget."

Static, static, the flag is lowered
and for a moment. . . love is the answer. . . static, static.

War against kids.
War against the weak and naïve.
War against the genuine and sincere.
War slaves follow the rhapsodic brass of policy,
the litany of fear, conspiracy, propaganda and patriotism.
It's always the battle of Jericho!
War to win the proudest grave,
the shiniest ring, the loudest rattle and darkest rose.
War for a lotto ticket in some bingo crucifixion.

Bring down the wall!
The trumpets call!

War in the cocaine filled nose of a Titan.
An alcoholic war to death on a fatal Playland metronome.

It's war we enjoy for the good of mankind.
A war of immutable truths.
An armchair siege against the insufferable moment.
With a cold beer, pill and an endorsement contract
we let the whole genetic act,
spatial twitch, contraction, eclipse, convulsion, reaction
take its epidemic course all the way home to faithful Penelope
weaving an atomic shawl.

Eventually resistance decays, the death of us all!
The wishbone and laurel create a placebo effect.
Self-control is a dog chasing its own tail.
War resumes.
In the name of war, faith exacts its own judgment.
In a cloud of dust.

Static.
Static.

War between The Joneses or Gonzalezes,
or whichever demographic elects the politicians these days.
It's not enough to simply keep up anymore,
to wear the trim and greenest lawn around our broken necks,
or to box the squarest hedge.
The journey to equality
is supplanted by war to surpass all wars,
to exceed and exterminate, dominate and destroy,
to flex and control, to own it all!

The winner must leave no bone unburned
or stone un-thrown.
In any line or lane, love is crushed underfoot on opening day.
On any shopping day.

War consumes us to possess any device and uselessness,
all of which become meaningless the moment they are
undressed or unpacked.

War to pay less, war to pay more.
Winning the bet.
Get out of my fucking way or I'll take your fucking head off!
I own this lamp, this dress, this house, this car, this road.
This highway destiny, this peak, this crest.
I am the metabolic genetic victor.
I own the spoils, the waste.
It is my right.
My reward
My religion running you down because
somewhere it says I can,
somewhere in some ancient testament,
some constitution,
it says I can stand my ground and so I must.
Somewhere in the constitution
it says winner takes all.
I am sure it does.
The right to war!

Static. Static.

War static, war static.

I hear that love is the answer, a quickly, extinguished sigh.

Then more static, war static.

Static.

War.

In my body, every nerve that permits
and justifies a fright and flight aggression,
unburned by a vestigial conscience.
There's a place for me
in *The Guinness Book of World Records*,
where future generations can read and know all about me.
I am the one who won the war.
Who ate the most all-beef hotdogs
in the least amount of time,
in a competition of consumptive gluttony,
one afternoon at some brutal county fair or rodeo,
the last rights festivity of squawking
chickens, grunting pigs and masticating cows.

War.

More war.

And before I am engraved in this record of Warrior Kings,
I must annihilate all trace of the future
to secure my eternal authority.
For I am god and nothing else.
The Great God Destroyer!
The last word always belongs to me.

The body and progeny is a meaningless task.
Only a means to the end,
and to know this is all that matters in the end.
Nothing needs to be left, not a seed or crust.

Who cares if I never sleep again?
Who cares about this approaching neuropathy?
The blisters on my brain?
I must go beyond that disease to extinction and annihilation.
With all my strength and breath,
The war is won only once the superior position is guaranteed
for the very last time,
and the last and loudest "fuck you" is mine.
An echo through the galaxy!
Not even that.
No, not even an echo. . .
Nothing remains.
Proof the war is finally won.

Static.

Static.

War.

Static.

Static.

More static.

I thought I heard her say, "Love is the answer."

Static.

But love is not enough.
The florist is a gladiator!

January 2013 - May 5, 2013, December 10, 2014

Terroristic

Downstream from the incinerated calamity
Wheat rises from a bone-yard exodus

        Sunset at Taiji Cove
        Satin monoxide corridors

          "I can't breathe!"

Migration of the armored cemetery
The ancient howling latitudes
Honey-shackled sunsets

    The pink eclipse at 4 a.m.

        Corrosive linguistic fakery
        Leaves spun on a static loom
        Ducklings in a petroleum eddy

Bellows wheeze in purple swollen light
Toxic figurines waltz over swollen graves
Swans of fire sail on a dying synapse

    Under the boughs of a blood division
    Hungry blades scorch the velvet harness

        Shit springs up from the ground
        Lithium worms wriggle through the clouds
        The skin of the gleaner's hands and feet
        Crack in the faint sun

Wisteria petals spill lavender on the pebble path
Hummingbirds roar through the radioactive forest
Beheadings and amputations float
In the coral shallows

     Insects click in the coiled iron prism of a nightmare
     Sticks gather in a furious bundle
     Beneath the broken willow

To tremble in the slaughter
To swim in atom light
To turn forever on a sleepless swell.

January 10, 2015

Free Ajami!

I've got to figure out
A better way to live my life
I've had enough

Twitch

Money
Money
Diamonds
Million dollar sequined gowns and bow ties
On the red carpet
Rock Stars who milk a revolution for golden knickers
Carry royalty's train
Court jesters
Clucking clowns
I smell a charity. . .
A mansion in The Bahamas loaded with real antiques
Blue money

Twitch
Twitch

What do you believe in?

They sing on
While syphilitic dictators suck the toxic oil tit
Like feeble Qatari emir Sheikh Hamad bin Khalifa Al Thani
Who sentenced poet Mohammed al-Ajami
to 15 years in prison

For reading a poem he proclaimed to be seditious
I spit on your name!

Impotent royalty
Gushes pus and cash from his ass
Injects *noblesse oblige* into France, reinvigorates
Disadvantaged slums, *mon ami*, blood money!
He turns his back to the god of justice and decency
Terrified by a poem!
Trembling in his halo!
What is it he wants?

Twitch
Twitch

Royalty is fiction
Madness cloaked in urine-soaked crowns of tradition
Cultural sycophants high on their own farts
Bankers who crush the heads of puppies
Politicians and movie stars nipped and tucked
Until there's nothing left
How did their souls die?

Sweaty sock puppets!
Playground bullies!
Official poets, playwrights, and scholars-for-hire
Impersonate the Classics
Dust and glue in Babel's ivory tower
Gatekeepers!
Masters and apprentices of the 21st Century
All slaves to corporate fiefdoms
Blowhard cartographers

Map emotion with an imperfect angle

Zombie billboards!
For 50 million dollars
The Pop Star spreads her legs for Coca-Cola
If *she* doesn't do it, somebody else will
The trot of radioactive flesh and bone
Branded eyelids of starlet silicone war machines
Strike a pose and hail the genocidal cock of industry
Paralyzed in paparazzi dildo camera lens
Thrilled by the rub of attention
A fool's version of life
That blinks and twitches
How do they sleep at night?
In sponsored straightjackets
The prize you win when you reach the top!
Lacerated wings and a pre-recorded message
Jingoistic brainwaves
A pinch collar
Lion meat!
Murderers in the Coliseum!
Star Gladiators!
Power whores!

Twitch

Irrelevant people have all the money
Interviewed on primetime just because they're rich
They must be geniuses
We have been reduced to a broad stroke

Twitch

Get ready for Mardi Gras
The electroshock revolution mounts
The albatross crashes through the roof
King Cake!
Don't choke on the plastic baby
Celebrate!
Espresso heavy with sugar and cream
Masks carved out of glitter and paste
The autoerotic bacchanalia begins
Mechanical floats lurch and
A Trojan Horse swings into step

Walk

Twitch

Walk

Twitch

Walk

St. Anne's to Treme
Here come the slaughtering blisters!
Hail, the fall from Grace!
Jewels fly from the balcony!
From Cairo, Egypt to chained Mississippi
"Tunisian Jasmine" recites in the air
Horns blow across The United Mexican States
100 Thousand Poets for Change assemble
In global communion

Twitch

The Seventh Seal
The Roman Catholic Pope abdicates the throne
He wants to spend more time in seclusion and prayer
Distance himself from sex abuse and corruption scandals
Papal infallibility is an urban myth
Who cares?
Oh, clockwork world!
Industrial conquest is not the cure-all
For poverty, racism and genocide
Freaks!
Rise up against the freaks!
Rednecks and steel guitars rise up for peace!
Hip-hop heads, schoolteachers, service industry employees
And trombonists rise up for peace!
Sleepers and other automatons snap out of it already!

Oh, clockwork world gloriously out of whack!
There's jazz on the border!
Mexican refugees beaten to death for throwing stones
At the Berlin Wall
Mothers and brothers and babies
Sacrificed by serial killers who never get caught
Who cares?
Decapitated and raped
Left in a ditch under a bough of weeping orchids and thorns
By soldiers, cops and other thugs
Insane with a hatred of god and beauty
Who brandish K-Y lubricated muzzles of assault rifles
Purchased from Whacko Apostles of

The Old Glory Church of The 2nd Amendment

There's a global warming protest in DC
I think I'll go!

Twitch

I spit on you and your name

Let me know when *you've* had enough

Twitch.

February 27, 2012

Welcome to Sonoma County

And the sleazy courts,
And the bribe-reaching police,
And the blood-loving generals,
And the money-loving preachers
Will all raise their hands against the kids who die,
Beating them with laws and clubs and bayonets and bullets . . .

— "Kids Who Die," Langston Hughes

The monster beauty moon rises over vineyards
Apple orchards, and ancient redwood forests

*

It's simple. It was murder
Andy Lopez was assassinated by a cop
One bullet in the heart killed him
The boy fell to the ground
6 more bullets followed
Then the police handcuffed his corpse

Remember Oscar Grant, Trayvon Martin, Michael Nida,
Yanira Serrano, Rigoberto Arceo, Kelly Thomas, Idriss Stelley,
Ernesto Duenez, Freddie Gray, Doug Zerby, Alan Blueford,
Michael Brown, Eric Garner, Tamir Rice, George Floyd, all
killed by police

5,000 people in the USA killed by police since 9/11
More than who died in the Iraq war

Tranquil and retired valleys, prosperous retreat
There's no better place for good people to live
than Sonoma County

On Friday, the crowd chanted "Jail him now!" as they
confronted riot police outside the courthouse. An effigy of
Sheriff Erick Gelhaus hung from a nearby light pole. "You
guys killed our friend, our cousin, our brother," shouted Lisbet
Mendoza, a Montgomery High student. "He was just a little
kid!"

Can poetry make death beautiful?

Just the few of us relax around the Russian River
Mammoth rubbings on sea stacks older than Jesus
Sea lions, vernal pools

When they realized he was just a boy
Carrying a toy gun
They gave him CPR

A sheriff's deputy shot and killed
a 13-year-old boy carrying a toy gun
A cop who fancied himself a gun expert, a war expert

A writer for S.W.A.T. magazine
A skilled killer took only a few seconds to come to judgment
On the life of little Andy Lopez

Erick Gelhaus executed an innocent child
There's no poetry in that

Hot tubs and spas, vegan foodies and star magic

When Gelhaus shouted out, Andy turned to his left and was
shot through the side, the bullet passed through his rib cage
and severed his aorta. According to police reports, it was
eleven seconds between the time that the sheriff called in to
headquarters and the killing.

Arnoldo Casillas, the Lopez Family attorney said, "More
crucial, in terms of the incident was the amount of time that
elapsed, between the time the sheriff called out and proceeded
to open fire. We do know that the important sequence, the
calling out a command to shooting, was just 2 to 3 seconds.
The two women in another car behind the patrol car said the
cops were shooting as they were getting out of the patrol car.
Andy wasn't given a chance to respond or react."

We planted an oak tree in Andy's memory
A few feet from where he was murdered
All the kids pitched in and everyone, his mom and friends
Wrote notes to Andy and put them in the ground with the tree

One bullet to the heart
One bullet in the back
Another bullet in the arm
Two bullets in the buttocks
One bullet in each wrist
One bullet in the neighbor's fence
At 3:15 p.m. on a beautiful fall day in southwest Santa Rosa
Andy was going to visit a friend after school
He was carrying a toy gun
When he was shot dead by Erick Gelhaus

> People here love their dogs, all kinds of poodles and doodles
> Lovely cats and agreeable parrots
> Occasionally, a boa constrictor

If a civilian makes a mistake and breaks the law
They go to jail
If a cop breaks the law in the United States of America
These big strong men and women
These big strong cops cry and cry
How being a cop is a terrible job

A horribly dangerous job
They cry and cry and clutch
Their guns, their Tasers, gas masks
Bullet proof vests, armored vehicles, sniper rifles, bayonets
They cry, these big strong cops, they cry
Because they feel threatened by a little boy
Threatened by a little boy with a toy gun
They kill little kids because they feel justified

And they go free!

They cry
How they love their pretty families
Love their country, law and order!
It's a dirty job, they cry, but someone has to do it
They are our heroes, the brutes,
stormtroopers, corporate police
Claim they're making a sacrifice for the good of us all
Freedom, they tell us, has a price
Child murderers collect their paychecks
Go home to their pretty families

They cry
They don't have time to think about justice
Weak ideals like justice, no time for silly ideals like justice
These trained assassins want our sympathy
Want to keep us in line
Want to kill us

Live oaks draped in sage lichens stagger low hills
Vintage rock & roll bands take you back to a day-glow time

These tough cops
Cry for more money and compassion
They need more guns to be more effective
Need tougher laws to be more effective
Need protection from the people
We can't be trusted

The cops are the thugs
Gangsters and terrorists
They want more prisons, bigger prisons for us
To put us in our place, a place for us
Indefinite detention, solitary confinement
They want to control us
Because we don't respect them
We can't be trusted
We are ungrateful, out of control
They want a system with more bullets
More walls, more laws
They want to freely execute justice
Execute little boys with toy guns
On a sunny day in southwest Santa Rosa

Fall harvest time for the stinky buds
Compassionate use in peaceful towns

Murderers with badges in black and blue
Go home to make love to their wives and husbands
Blood on their hands
Caress each other in the bloody dark
Smear and smother each other in bloody love

With blood on their hands
The blood they want to call love
They play ball with their kids, cradle their babies
With blood on their hands
They walk their children to school
Bound by blood

Their bullets tear through
The hearts of innocent children
Just doing their job
They go home to their families
Kiss and grope each other
Hands stained with innocent blood
The blood they want to call love

The Sonoma Plein Air Art Festival
The Harmony Festival

Hearts rotten with angry justice
Tongues rotten with terroristic lies
Official murderers in black and blue
Who spend their working hours
Bullying the poor, black, Latino kids
Anyone they want
Whenever they want
They are the law
Keep the law
Make the law

With a license to kill
They stop and frisk without probable cause
Strike fear in the hearts of us all
Just because they can
"Keep the niggers down"

And we obey them
We are their niggers

Their field niggers
Their peasant Jews
Still under the boots of robocops
They break down our doors
Beat us up in our homes
Answer our emergency calls for help
With a stick and gun and a fist
Rape us, kill us, break our bones
Murder our children
They are the law
These bullies with blood on their hands
Hate and fear in their hearts

"Kids will be kids,"
the cops say when their children get out of line
When our children get out of line they are assassinated

What a great morning for a hot air balloon classic!

Walking in our school clothes to play
Cowboys and Indians, cops and robbers
Just like on television
In our innocent daylight clothes
They shoot us dead

And when there's an outcry from the public
When a mother clutches the bullet-riddled corpse of her baby
When a father will never see his child again
When a family is destroyed
The police investigate the police

And the story ends there. . .

"I'm lonely living without my son," Sujey Lopez said. "I need
my son in my life."

The District Attorney, funded by cops, reviews
The investigation of cops done by cops
There is no poetry in that

> *Wild berry lanes, fresh crab at Bodega Bay*
> *Where Hitchcock filmed the fantasy horror film "The Birds"*

I believe there's a war against the people

Armed to the teeth
They tell us with stone eyes
The death of the child is "collateral damage"
The cops, the law and order folks
Cite extenuating circumstances
As they murder us in our homes
Bludgeon us on the streets
In our playgrounds and parks

This is how it really is
What will it take to get through to you?

> *The Luther Burbank Home & Garden*
> *The Charles M. Schultz Museum*

The police apologists say, "The cop felt threatened.
What would you do if you were a cop?"

The slavish apologists say,
"You would have killed that little boy too, right?"

Campaign fundraisers
Pasta feeds, crab feeds, pancake feeds
Calm and abundance, take a cooking class, play golf

"Jailhouse for Gelhaus!"
The murdering cop is on administrative leave
(Now he's back on the streets)
He will get his retirement bonus
Andy Lopez is dead forever

"No Justice, No Peace!"

Yes, you should have seen
The stormtroopers at the Sonoma County Sheriff's Office
How they greeted our babies
Kids who came peacefully to demonstrate
Express their sadness and fear
About the killing of their little friend
They were greeted by snipers, behind barriers, tear gas
Brutality and force as an answer to grief
A lesson from bullies in the most teachable moment
This, their first lesson in democracy!

Blue jays, mystery-grilled mushrooms
California Sister butterflies in the morning
make you glad to be alive

*

We are purified by good actions, I say
I want my life back! I say
Will I ever find rest from this nightmare of police brutality?

One of Andy's friends screams, "Gelhaus, you will cry
like a Mexican baby when they lock your crying ass up in a
jail cell for 20 years"

What does President Obama think
about the murder of a 13-year-old boy?
He's too busy killing 13-year-old boys in Pakistan
to think about Andy Lopez

The apathy gene is missing in the sociopath

Gelhaus says, "turn on the mean gene"

While the wound is open we have to do surgery
The sickness is systemic, remove the rotten flesh
The shattered bone, punish the guilty
Cure the bully psychosis
Then we can focus on healing

*

Someone screams, "Fuck the police!"

And a child crosses the police line

Someone screams, "Fuck the police!"

Kids are getting beaten, harassed, shot by the police

Someone screams, "Fuck the police!"

A legitimate expression in the face of oppression

They are angry, yes, and have a right to be

Someone screams, "Fuck the police!"

Yes, a baby boy was shot in the heart
Two blocks from his home
On a sunny suburban day
Gelhaus was never at risk
He could have called in for backup
He was showing off

Andy Lopez was executed
In 11 seconds
Gelhaus got out of his car
Shot Andy Lopez 7 times
Handcuffed Andy's dead body

Gave the corpse (Andy) CPR
Then called in "shots fired"
In 11 seconds

Someone screams, "Fuck the police!"

Latinos and blacks and whites tell their true-life stories

Someone screams, "Fuck the police!"

No, I won't be winning any poetry contests
with words like these

Someone screams, "Fuck the police!"

No lovely meditations on arrogant Renaissance constructions

Someone screams, "Fuck the police!"

No musings on gold tapestries and clever forms

Someone screams, "Fuck the police!"

No nice cupolas
no elegant verse and carefully placed metaphors

Someone screams, "Fuck the police!"

A father calls the police to report that his son stole his van
He wants to teach his son a lesson
But the boy would not heed the policeman's "lawful demands"
So, the police shot him dead

Someone screams, "Fuck the police!"
Someone screams, "Fuck the system!"
Someone screams, "Fuck the president!"
Someone screams, "Fuck the corporations!"
Someone screams, "Fuck the military!"
Someone screams, "Fuck the politicians!"

And fuck the NSA who have joined us
here for this intimate moment of poetry
I know you are watching

No poetry with well-articulated parlor room niceness
Thanksgiving is coming soon
No, I won't be celebrating genocide

Someone screams, "Fuck the Mayflower"
Someone screams, "Fuck the Pilgrims"

It was murder. Andy Lopez was executed

Someone screams, "Fuck the police!"
Someone screams, "Fuck westward expansion"

And fuck what they did to the Plains Indians
and the buffalo slaughterers and the fucking Alamo

"Asesinos!"

Someone screams, "Fuck the Alamo!"
Someone screams, "Fuck Christopher Columbus!"
Someone screams, "Fuck the conquistadors

for killing and raping the Indians of Central America"
Someone screams, "Fuck the United States flag"
Someone screams, "Fuck all flags!"
And someone screams, "I don't support our troops"
Someone screams, "I don't support the *mean gene*"
Someone screams, "I don't support the 21st century
Pinkertons!"

And fuck the police, fuck the president,
fuck the prison industrial complex,
the military industrial complex,
fuck the self-appointed authorities of capital

Someone screams, "Fuck the slavemasters!"

We will not be painting the trees pretty colors
We will paint the air black with our voices

> *Under the redwoods and lush winter rain*
> *After a Reiki massage and tabouli salad*

Someone screams, "Fuck the police!"

There must be justice for Andy!
There must be justice now!

One freezing night in the Valley of the Moon
Candles and prayers, signs, more signs
We take to the street

I scream, "Fuck the police!"

*

The monster beauty moon rises over vineyards
Apple orchards, and the ancient redwood forest. . .

The Trumpeters

Cowards in white sheets, the skinhead cops
and racists, the religious working men
and women who think a woman's place is
in the kitchen and children are to be seen
and not heard, and believe people of color
are here in America as a privilege, not a right,
who blame Obama for 9/11, but he wasn't
even president then, the ones who say racism
didn't exist in America until Obama,
the blowhards, The Trumpeters, the ones
who will murder to be in the driver's seat
of a big white capitalist car, who will never
be in the driver's seat, will always be
second-rate white people, in the rich
man's eye, they might as well be black
for their marginalized existence in the grand
scheme of the upper-class American
power elite, but still they buy into the lie,
with their heads up the ass of the real oppressors,
the powerful whites who will never share
a piece of the pie with their middle-class
and working class, poor white cousins, who
only see these ordinary folk, these regular
people as grist for the mill, unruly ignorants
who they can use to help them build their
oligarchic empires, the front line of their
marching band, The Trumpeters, blowing
the horn of oppression, blowing the horn
of the white man's dream to rule the world,

the white man's dream to carry guns
in the street, free to murder kids in Sandy Hook,
free to beat their wives, and practice rape
as a contact sport while they graduate
from Stanford University with a big white
degree, free to treat a woman as property,
like a piece of shit, these Trumpeters, they blow,
and blow hard, The Trumpeters, the 40 percent,
maybe 50 percent of America, who will sell
their souls for the promise of ever-elusive
power, the good old Christians who spit
in Christ's face and rape him on the cross,
the ones that covet cruelty, The Trumpeters,
the patriotic Trumpeters, the ones who think
the USA is a page in an owner's manual,
clear as day, that they can own democracy,
rig and twist justice and truth to their
self-interested lies and aspirations, that justice
can be bought and sold, as long as white
people rule the world, The Trumpeters,
the ones who think the USA is a big fucking
TV set, as they slurp down their supersized
cans of pharmaceutical sugar and poison,
The Trumpeters, who mimic some hallmark
illusion of The Great White American Way,
and lick the boots of a reality show star,
The Trumpeters, may they suffer the pain
they wish on the poor, the weak, the abandoned,
and rot in the hell of their own vanity,
greed, envy, pride, lust, gluttony, sloth and ten
more sins that are their legacy, the sins of
The Trumpeters! Oh, Trumpeters, come on,

blow, blow, blow, your trumpets, here
comes your monster daddy, he comes to give
you another script to read because you can't
think for yourselves, and he will fuck you
in the ass, and he will never kiss you, never
ever be like you, or with you, he will only
bleed you, and bleed you, fodder for his wars,
fodder for his ecocidal factories, fodder
for his machineries of deception, yes, you
will be his robot army, because you are,
accept it, only Trumpeters, only soulless slaves,
at your very core, behind your brassiness
you are only a procession of cowards, and you
will follow and pronounce your yahoo
independence as you walk to your hate-filled
grave, you will follow the goosestep of the
high boot and genocide, get in line proud
Trumpeters, the future is yours, there's a banquet
waiting for you beyond the gates of Valhalla,
come on, you are the lucky ones, the entitled ones,
not only the desired guest for the feast, you are
the feast itself, so bow down and open your collar,
your red-haired father is coming to devour you.

Ode to the Deniers

You can gas the Jew
Hang the black man
Deport the Mexican
Annihilate the Muslim
Beat up the queer
and leave them to die
on a barbed wire fence

You can wage another war
Another good ol' World War
Starve and maim a million or two
People will scream and cry
Bleed and turn to dust
in the flames
of a manufactured death
But don't worry, we'll be okay
It's nothing new
We suffer and die to be born again
That's what humans do

Though maybe this time
it will be different
Maybe this time
it's a better game you play
You pull the plug
on the ecological bathtub
Drain the primordial swamp
Scorch the fragrant air
Electrify the crystal water

Dissolve the loamy land
Suck the life out of it all
Stoke the fires of vanity,
fires that end the unholy
reign of humans on this
irreparable Planet Eden

Yes, maybe this time
it will be different
Maybe this time
you've done much better
in all of your green-ending glory
Maybe you've done it at last
Completely achieved
your murderous direction
Torn us from our budding homes
Ripped us from our final flesh
Extinguished the soul of light

Yes, maybe this time
you've finally done it
Finally made your mark
And we can say to you,
in praise and approbation,
Congratulations, Deniers!
You have finally won
your blessed Armageddon.

November 23, 2016

Wrecking Crew After Parkland

We came with a wrecking crew
And wrecked ourselves
Which wrecked the world

We marched with blades of iron
Prayed in crushing things
And gave ourselves a static silence

We claimed the earth with dirty bombs
And all the living turned to suffering
And we were strangers here

We sanctified a cultural robbery
Drunk with calamity and guns
And blew our lungs wide open

We stormed a diaphanous future
Hailing armor-piercing bullets
Murdered children at their lessons

We came with a wrecking crew
And wrecked ourselves
Which wrecked the world

And we were none the wiser.

November 16, 2017 - March 22, 2017

War Hawks

If standing on a pile of corpses
waving a flag makes you feel less ashamed
of being a murderer, go for it, War Hawks,
wave those flags! A new shipment of bodies
will arrive in the morning just for you

If it will make you feel better about the death
of your sons and daughters, husbands, uncles,
aunts, cousins, and friends, who over the years
have fought in the army, marines, air force
and navy, wave that flag, and remember them.
Wave that flag and rejoice in the celebration
of enemies vanquished and wars won.

Come to the tarmac, War Hawks,
wave your flags as black body bags
issue from the bellies of shiny jets,
the second birth of the fallen innocent.
Come to the tarmac, War Hawks,
where boxes of bloody limbs roll down
the conveyor belt, for transfer
to a sorting center where surgeons
will match up twitching hands and feet,
dismembered arms and legs,
and pulsing stumps aching for a complete
and perfect life in the name of freedom
and justice. And when that quilt
of torn flesh is rebuilt and ready,
you can go down to the place where

death is stored to identify your
very own Frankenstein monster.

Wave on, War Hawks!
Here comes a tub of disembodied bowels
Buckets of brains, bloodless veins, and kidneys
Organs of memory, and silent nerves
Come sing your patriotic songs!
Rejoice with verve and wave your flags
for the greater good. Commemorate
the killing, for if you don't have
your killing, you won't have your heroes
and without your heroes you won't have
a reason to justify your sorrow.

Madrigal

(The USSR Journals, 1990)

Russian Renaissance

for Galina

Can I hold the wind together?
Crescent arm around your waist
Though bodies here are second place
What is the Cobalt Lesson?

Travelers in eight tongues
Collide, a dozen hands in discourse
Wave and light fuse
Poems, fruits accumulate

Without line or static wait
Dreams dissipate in caution
Can I bind essentialities?

In a basket on the table
Can I press my tongue to fact?
That flesh and mind are agitprop
Spirit all an afterthought

That separates wrong from right
That hop and wait
While others watch us drink
What lovers need to think

Can I hold the wind together?
As you in pointing measure
Lead futurists to meet the future
Singing madrigals and rounds

Pointing statuesque
Lenin's child in handmade dress
Will we arm a common fate?
Can I hold the wind together?

CCCP

for my mother

1.

History disarms armies
Ill-equipped to march, heroes
wait in line. Fat drips
The last chicken on Arbat St.

Big as life, Kremlin
Big as life, window
View from Intourist Hotel

May Day flags on the boulevard
Gymnasts in Red Square. Red trees
about to bloom under Red
portrait of Lenin

(Lenin embalmed by The Immortalization Committee)

Moneychangers on the floor
of The Georgian Restaurant
Shashlik sours my stomach
I wash down *perestroika* with kvass

The KGB in our hotel room
Don't explain themselves
But stay until the parade is over

Buy Russian Bread with jam

Dine in Jewish co-op with Trotsky mural
Walk with thousands into Red Square
To watch changing of the guard at Lenin's tomb

Lose $10 hard currency in Spanish slot machine

Watch fireworks from Lenin Hills
Watch Gorbachev on television

Visit convent
Then a Jewish synagogue
My mother puts money in the donation box

K.G.B. Headquarters
Gorky Park
Armand Hammer's new hotel
Cemetery of Khrushchev and Mayakovsky

Get tickets for *Nutcracker Suite* at The Bolshoi

I feel queasy all day

2.

Packed and ready by 4 a.m.
Go to Sochi

MOTHER: I got up at 1, 2, 3. Finally at 5:30 got dressed.
           My good nature (ha! ha!) returned when I was
           handed a plastic bag with a bottle of water,
           cheese sandwich & lo & behold a salami

sandwich. I deposited it in the nearest ash can. We shlepped into a large airplane surrounded by a bunch of foreigners, who didn't shut their mouths talking loudly to overcome the music, also in a foreign language I've begun to hate with all my heart and soul.

Tea groves
Yew trees
Daguys
Coffee's thick foam
sticks to the rim

Worry about the price of hotel laundry service

Deep in Kandinsky

NANCY: Kandinsky is a friend living beside my head. I understand his heart's desire although I don't live creation like him - me - tread water not afraid I'll drown. I'll get to the middle of the horizon where the picture is clearest. I'd rather not paint than do a conscious rational plan.

*

DREAM: A spot glows on the stone floor of a cave-like cottage. I'm with an old fisherman and his black-haired daughter. They are both very nice

and I promise to return. Then his daughter runs
me over with her car and drives away

*

Skip stones on Black Sea
Vegetable gardens on the footpath
Up to the monstrous Dagomys Hotel
I get lost in the elevators

Two women follow us to our room
They offer Nancy rubles for her clothes
She isn't interested
They see peanut butter crackers on the table
They want to buy them
Nancy gives them each a pack
And asks them to leave

Two pigeons on the balcony
Valley of tea groves
Train tracks on smooth stone beach

Akhmatova souvenir photos in Sochi bookstore
A fresh baked cinnamon roll for 25 kopeks

BRUCE: Why prolong the anticipation? Eat cheese, peas
           and potatoes from the plate of others who can
           spare it. Chicken Kiev, not the city—the
           Chicken.

My brother Bruce doesn't eat meat
Says he's starving
Because there's no fish or vegetables

My mother makes *me* ask the waiter for caviar
The near-sighted waiter says there is no caviar
"I am sure they have caviar," mother tells me
I ask the waiter four more times
The fourth request brings the manager

MOTHER: My son is starving.
          There's nothing here for him to eat.
          He must have caviar!

The manager brings Bruce black market caviar
Bruce wants everyone to join him
Mother, Nancy and I decline, full of Chicken Kiev
Bruce insists, so Nancy and I each eat a spoonful of caviar

This makes Bruce happy

Drunk on vodka, Bruce and Nancy dance Armenian disco

3.

Sochi to Kiev

PROPAGANDA: "Anything that isn't forbidden by law is
              legal."

We walk out on the runway

A bus of Soviet passengers are parked in front of the plane
We're escorted to the head of the line and board

Think about a massage I had in Sochi
The best part was when he squeezed my hands
So hard my knuckles popped

6:30 sunrise
No cameras or binoculars permitted on the plane

Kiev
Apple blossoms, smog
79 years ago my grandmother
left here for the U.S.

"XXth Century and Peace"
"Green" revolution

Kiev downwind from Chernobyl

Earthmen beware of the apples!

Granite arch by Dnieper River
Commemorates end of Nazi occupation

Kiev is the oldest city, 1023 A.D.

Farming, manufacturing
It says in a brochure—*The Ukraine*

A fly on the table in Dnieper Hotel
This room is damp and cold

Nancy exercises
I've got a sore throat

Soviet Union short on vegetables and fish
Vegetarians eat bread, rice, cabbage, canned peas

Utopian experiments
Bridges fail
A good war might give direction—
"Star Wars—Defense or Aggression"

Orange phone with a black cord rings
I answer but there's no one there
My Russian teacher in America said
This has something to do with KGB

The dining room is huge
The elevator is tiny

Big bird's nest in the forest
Birch trees everywhere

On the boulevard, near the city center
The tree trunks are painted white

Kandinsky retrospective in Moscow
Warhol retrospective in New York

The world is coming to an end
Swan Lake in Kiev

*

Today we take a day trip to Kanev
Kanevsky, is my grandfather's name
Nadia is our tour guide

Puzhalsta, spasiba

Television *pa Ruski*

3 coffees

What have I got in my hand?
Kopeks

Horse chestnut
Maple, lilac
Pyramidal poplar trees
Oak, fir
Horse chestnut
On Kiev coat of arms

Gold Star—Hero City—W.W. II
77 days defending against the Germans

Beech trees, black birch
White acacia, yellow acacia
Linden trees for icon stands

Kiev on the banks of Dnieper
The third largest river in Europe

Chemical plants downstream
Upstream concrete wall
Stops ground water seepage
From Chernobyl

"1964-1985 The Stagnation Period"
"Pluralism of Opinion"

Storks interrupt a political discussion

Winter wheat, buckwheat
Sugar beet, sunflowers, peas
Black rye bread with pork fat

NADIA: If you want good food, eat at home.

Storage
Transportation
Distribution
Soviet economic problems

After Lenin, philosophy developed
Separate from society

Ukranian Zones
Kanev is in the Steppe Zone
Rolling steppes to Black Sea
Black soil zone

10th century Byzantine influence
Kiev-Rus
Blown glass, ceramics, lace

Wood carving

Kobzar

16th century Cossacks
Blinded by Turks while in prison
Wandered with bandura and sang of a heroic past
They earned money as beggars
Ordinary feudal peasants
They occasionally raided the landlords

1861 serfdom abolished

Lenin, Lenin, Lenin. Lenin
Lenin, Lenin. Lenin, Lenin
Lenin. Lenin, Lenin, Lenin

Taras Shevchenko Museum
Revolutionary poet 1814-1862
Spent 25 years as a serf
10 years exiled in Czar's Siberian army
Forbidden to write during exile
Hid poetry in his boots
Secretly drew 400 pictures

Buried in his dear Ukraine
When Taras died
The people carried his body by cart
From village to village
Hundreds of miles
So all could pay homage

With bad breath, and a script that took months to learn
The Vice-Chairman of Taras Museum
Escorts us through endless rooms of exaltation
We study reproductions

NADIA: Taras was much appreciated
                because he was so close to the people.

Later when I ask her if we can detour
From the permitted route of our day trip
She wants to know why

ME: I want to be close to the people.

Down Taras Hill through mountain ash

"My Testament"

We eat lunch in a narrow room
Borsch, Azerbaijani sweet red wine
Cucumbers, salami, varenikes
Pork cutlets, potato, cucumbers
Mayonnaise, salami, mineral water

The history continues
They invade, destroy
City, art
Czar
Mosaics

Built, built, built. . .

Natural mummification
Oak trees in orchards, dandelions
Hooligans
Feathers on roasted chicken

Lenin Museum

City Gates
Universities
Unions
Clubs
Party

Lenin, Lenin, built. . .

St. Sophia built by Yaroslav The Wise
Wise men rebuild Yaroslav
From bones in the yard
At Kiev Pechersk Lavra
I pay 75 cents for a Fanta with an American dollar
And get three chocolates in gold coin wrappers for change

Mother, Nancy and I have a cold

My mother didn't like Kiev

MOTHER: I heard the voices of my forefathers
                 tell me about the pogroms.

4.

Going to Leningrad

A big fat pushy lady in a red scarf smiles
Stinks up the airplane seat beside me
It's the same pushy lady from the hotel
Who barreled into the elevator and made me sneeze

In a window seat, I feel confined
Bleary double plastic window
Rain outside
I swallow a cold pill without water
Sour sticks to my throat

The fat lady is still smiling

And the guy we met in Maxim's last night
Slips 40 rubles in my hand
He's going back to L.A
And it's a non-convertible currency

Nazdorovye, Tovarich!

I straddle the fat lady to get a glass of water
She still stinks and smiles
She points at her seat belt
I buckle my seat belt

Nazdorovye, fat lady!

Red scarf, white blouse
Black shirt, gold tooth

Her husband
in a gray suit on the aisle

Taxi Aeroflot
1 hour 30 minutes
Kiev to Leningrad

The Fat Lady powders her nose for takeoff

Farewell again, Kiev-Rus
Your steppes bleed with potato juice!

The fat lady genuflects
Closes her eyes
We take off

                    *

            Soviet Lies

    1. Are those nuclear power plants I see there?
     NO

    2. Can we visit a small village on our way back from
    Kanev?
    YES

3. Pollution is made by man, therefore not so bad,
symbolizes effort to achieve through technology

In the air the Fat Lady is very nice
She gets me mineral water from the stewardess

4. Afghan war was to protect Afghanistan from
Pakistan and U.S.

5. We acknowledge crimes of Stalin and plurality of
opinion

Nuclear chimneys

Soviets claim
England exports acid rain
To Sweden
The U.S. to Canada
Acid rain Soviet-style
Is rain of the people

ME: Don't you ever get sick of Lenin's face?

NADIA: Shevchenko monument built
           because he was close to the people

But she won't let me get close to the people

Hitching a ride home from the ballet

DRIVER: I don't want your money. You are friends,

Amerikansky!

Our tour guide's opinions
Not derived from plurality of thinking
Always thinking dialectical
She was impressed I read Mayakovsky
Shot himself in the heart
Just in time to be immortalized

100. Mayakovsky shot himself

False teeth of George Washington
Carved like linden icon stands

Peace means we are in agreement
Until the next war—

Peace—
For the green Revolution

Liars honestly believe their lies
Believers honestly invested
In nu-speak church of stagnant years

Let me guide you—
Kiev, occupied two years—
Hero city fought and won

We'll speak of Lenin later—

After Stalin—
Singly responsible for the murder of

20, 30, 40 million —
Praised Lenin to divert attention
From his wicked self—

These misguided Soviet lambs—
Serfs, slaves
All the time thought Stalin was Lenin—

Religious persecution?
Assassination?
Social Realism?—

Who is the killer?
Liar beast?

Facsimile Museum!
People not loving!
Future not the future
Only fucking Radiance Philosophy!

Khrushchev rehabilitated in 1988
1000 Congregations of God now in operation
God praise our atheistic state!

Why praise?

Lenin
Lenin
Lenin

Isn't the only policy the best policy?

Is memory being forgotten?

*

The nice fat lady fixes her make-up for landing

Leningrad

5.

How to contend with

    Czar?

    or

Kiev Pechersk Lavra—
60,000 Serfs for God

Russian Byzantine 11th century
Russian Baroque 18th century

    Frescoes
      of
    St. Sophia

Yaroslav The Wise
Buried with some woman

In a tomb of marble from the Black Sea

I hate secrets!

Kandinsky said that red means Joy

*

My mother has pneumonia
We take her to a hospital, in an ambulance
With Leonid, the young Jewish doctor
Who has a Groucho Marx moustache

LEONID: Don't worry, be happy.

MOTHER: Are you Jewish?

LEONID: No, I am Russian.

MOTHER: You are not Russian, you are Jewish

LEONID: Yes, I am Jewish. Don't worry, be happy.

My mother says the sheets are stained and dirty
Stuffing oozes from the naugahyde bed
Leonid tells us this hospital is the best
It's for tourists and chief party members
My mother refuses to stay
Opts for immediate return to the U.S.A.
While the nurse takes her blood pressure

She looks out the window to a graveyard

MOTHER: That's where they bury their mistakes.

*

May 9th Victory Day celebration
Nazis defeated
Survivors, Press, flowers
Venetian cumulus, 1941-1945

Six hours changing tickets
Documents for travel
Nancy and I stay in Leningrad
Bruce goes home with my Mother

Helsinki to Miami

*

The Delivery

Nancy and I call the families
Of our Russian friends
Who live in America

We deliver packages
Cigarettes, toothpaste, aspirin

Hermitage (Part 1)

Escorted through back door by guide
Through dark hall tapestries
White room where Kerensky's
provisional Government fell—
October, 1917

Malachite, columns, chandeliers
Filigree, gold leaf, mosaic
Sienna, Rembrandt, parquet

Vaulted ceilings
Marble balustrades
Porcelain antiquities
Crimean mother of urns

Marble death of Pygmalion and Galatea
White toes bit by scorpion
El Greco, Velasquez, Boy and Dolphin

Heart of Russia

Trident of orange and gold horses
Tug Eastern Nights to Europe
Irina and Tsar Nikita's daughters end autocracy
Paul's succession

*

In Soviet Union 1989 Perestroika
U.S.A. awakens from Reagan stagnation

Under the stars of a white night
On the canal by Mars field
20 kopeks and a wish

Health to Leningrad!

*

Chernika - blue bilberry juice
1 a.m., Nancy brushes stain from her tongue

Visit Vodka store with Ravil

MAN IN LINE: "Why don't you show Americans the
                          toilet where we go to drink our vodka."

I'm not sure what he means.

Egg Salad, black bread
Chicken, potatoes, sardines
Waffles stuffed with custard
Georgian mineral water

George, my Russian teacher's ex-husband
comes to visit with a woman who doesn't eat

GEORGE: I will emigrate to U.S.A. in August!

He complains about low wages
Product shortages

Ravil promises to give the shoes
I brought from U.S.A. to Inga
So, she can get married. . .

Russian Museum

Icons
Rublev

Visit prison
St. Peter and Paul's Fortress

Peter the Great enjoyed pulling teeth

                         *

101. No one has ever escaped from Peter and Paul's Fortress

ME: Who was Kropotkin?

                    *

St. Isaac's Cathedral
Pride of tragic Montferrand
Hermitage (Part 2)

Impressionists
Blue painting of Akhmatova
Akhmatova calendars in the bookstore
I buy five of them

Dinner at Leonid's apartment
His passport says Jew as nationality
He is prepared to leave to Israel or U.S.A.
In the Fall. After dinner, Leonid
walks us to our hotel

Figures in white night twilight wait for a bus

Siren
Blue light
Police on motorcycles

We say goodbye at the door
Of Hotel Pulkovskaya
Russians not allowed in

In the hall, outside our room
A U.S. film crew smokes cigarettes
Listens to blues
Films a documentary

*

Petrodvorets tour with a guide
Palace of Peter The Great
Rebuilt after Nazi occupation
Nothing but rubble left

Time bombs. . .

Gold fountains

Find more Akhmatova calendars for sale

10 a.m.
Ravil on the telephone
He wants me to bring Galina
A Soviet National Songbook

RAVIL: There are many things, many problems I want
            to say but cannot because my English not

Every friend wants a letter from the U.S.A.
Today the Soviets still write letters
They say it would be different if they had telephones

    Dear Jim,

    Latest from Leningrad, Hotel Angleterre destroyed.
    Hotel Astoria under renovation. Esenin rumored to be
    murdered by Stalin. Many wish to exhume his body. I
    think this is an error. I think it was Mayakovsky. . .

Rain purges the exhausted Leningrad air
Nancy and I go to Moscow to catch a plane home
Troops withdrawn in Czechoslovakia
American president tells Soviets to continue with Perestroika

6.

Lenin by Violet
Yaroslav to Golden Gates
Ajar

Ships come down
The Strontium River

Flood every epoch

With a fairy tale
Of daughters
Suckling
Shackled father

I take a fist of hair
From the tail of a monster
Who pulls a thousand-wheeled cart

Lenin, Lenin, Lenin

Marble by moonlight

Every hour

Changing guard. . .

Dagovich

Dagovich. . .

He started to use fine stationary. His letters grew longer and longer. He describes the fruitcake on the polymer tablecloth. Lives in a three-bedroom, two and a half bath house in Pacifica. A Japanese tea garden, raku kiln, 28,000 sq. ft. of greenhouse or nine buildings, not including packing sheds, aluminum boiler buildings and three-fifths of a barn that blew apart seven years earlier.

We could begin here but think of Russian mornings.

70% of them were factual, the rest underpaid, to be a Jew wasn't ordinary but an engineer or doctor. One day in the past, near Leningrad, his grandfather put tefillin on his head, and said a prayer.

The players, tall, wore placards, said, "Workers Wanted." though when the Jews showed up for work, Weisman, Dagovich, Kanevsky, no workers were needed. Thank you, Mr. Black Man of Russia, Estonia, Caucasus. Meld in Byelorussia.

A list of names tattooed on the inside of his eyebrows.

Date another form. San Mateo cultural Exchange Bureau. Food stamps. Medi-Cal registration.

Blinis cook in the kitchen.

At the Big Salad Bar: tuna, salmon salad, mushrooms, corn, garbanzo beans, macaroni salad, (no beets on the menu), topped with sunflower seeds. Russian dressing renamed Thousand Island dressing. Croutons. Chicken soup. Onion soup. Chili. Root Beer.

Is there a place for the stomach in history?

Laughing child, father, mother. Fog, the first time as it settles into Pacifica valleys. They have nothing. Play tag. Play ball with the dog. I down sedatives because life is too exciting.

What is it?

"An unreal thing."

Unreal?

"Yes, Russian food in America."

Dagovich. . .

Whose grandfather would sneeze 17 times every day, while he only sneezes seven. It's not an allergy or cold. Who plays piano, won competition in Soviet Union when fifteen. His mother had tears over her face. It was a great day. Still he plays in Vienna awaiting transfer to Italy. Finally, in America, he goes to meet caseworker from Jewish Vocational Service to see about a doctor's license. Soviet credentials a meaningless thing. Questions in English. Who speaks so little English, can hardly explain, except Mozart is his favorite composer.

Who discovers himself in a delivery van. Delivers bromeliads for sale in mail order catalogue at Mission warehouse. It's new, all very new. Social Security cards in the mail today, first letter received at U.S.

address, three cards and welcome to Social Security. Who will ride Bay
Area Rapid Transit system from Market and 5th to Daly City. Will
call when he gets there. I'll pick him up.

Now I wait for him. . .

In May of 1990, my mother, brother, Nancy traveled to
the Soviet Union. In Leningrad mother got pneumonia. The
hotel called the hospital, then Leonid Dagovich arrived in an
ambulance.

My mother's room.

"Don't worry, be happy," Meher Baba wisdom from
Soviet doctor with thick moustache, bright dark eyes.

"Don't worry, be happy!"

Mother asked him if he's Russian.

"Yes," he said.

"No, you're not Russian."

"I am."

She says, "Are you Jewish?"

"Yes."

"I knew you weren't Russian."

My mother returned to the U.S. for medical care. In the days following, five days in Leningrad, Nancy and I had dinner with Leonid and his family.

Leonid now Leo, his wife, Yevgenya, now Jane, daughter Margarita, now Maggie. Mother and father of Jane stay behind. Leonid has a great-grandmother who is 92, "sick in the head because of her age."

Leonid took me to a synagogue, showed me Smolny Institute, Leningrad Conservatory of Flowers, and the place where he grew up. He was planning to leave in December, but didn't know where he wanted to go. He did not want to go to Israel, though his sister lived there, because of fighting with Arabs. He could get ten thousand dollars to move to South Africa, or Australia. He wanted most to live in the U. S., but didn't have a sponsor. It required a sponsor. San Francisco was where many Soviet refugees went. There's a political distinction between immigrant and refugee. According to Hebrew Immigrant Aid Society, an immigrant "enters", a refugee "flees to escape well-founded fear of persecution due to race, religion, national origin or political beliefs."

Jew. . .

The U.S. government determines the refugee. Honduras. Guatemala. U.S. supplies right wing El Salvador with aid. Left wing opposition murdered. Any opposition murdered. These people aren't considered refugees, they're considered immigrants. Denied entrance, deported, held in safe houses, hidden in churches in American cities by do-gooders, fellow travelers, for fear Immigration and

Naturalization Service will send them back to right wing juntas, in power, funded by. . . .

Leonid, with support, Jew, HIAS. Mrs. Doris Rothenberg provides sponsorship grant.

Sometimes I feel like a child, but that's okay, then no one can blame me. Going back in time. Another story sets sail from Leningrad, Byzantium, Peter the Great. Ugly story of right way, in the grip of wrong man in ill wind. A table cut from a slice of red wood, a maple tree in Kiev.

Vermont syrup on French toast. Saturday morning cartoons. Margarita understands children have all the fun. Parents get jobs, when they get a job. When Jewish Vocational Service picks up two leads, one from Radio Free Europe at $5.75 an hour, no benefits, no weekends. "We'd love to have a doctor here." The geriatric and insane convalesce in Linda Mar. A beautiful hospital. Eucalyptus air. Cypress. Dried out potted plants.

Cynical. . .

Waking Nancy. Have to get up before 7 a.m. It's not my fault. I was born in America. Why should I get up? Leonid has appointment with a doctor, job to draw blood, nine dollars an hour. He gets to look at patients. Only look. I've never been a refugee before.

Dagovich is me. . . .

94

Leonid starts work today. Think about it. If you were running a business, needed a lab technician and CETA was bankrupt, full of the depraved, you'd call an agency like Jewish Vocational Service, find a Soviet doctor who can't practice, but is willing to work cheap.

West wind in the window. Water like a washing machine sloshing in window of a seventeen-story dream.

Drive to work, drive back. Bus schedules. Bromeliads for hotel sitters. Come to buy ten boxes of Spanish Moss. Ellen probably has breast cancer in New York. She talks to a pathologist, the son of my next-door neighbor for twenty some years.

We must help Dagovich, get him on his feet. That's enough to do. Run for city council. Poet, environmentalist, social type with a capital slant, here on this hill. Crystal Springs Reservoir by which someone gets drinking water to wash teeth.

Willy Wonka's Chocolate Factory. Massage. Dr. Oberstein, Leonid's new boss calls about second night of Passover.

Ur-Family up to it. Cyndi Lauper. Ur-Pop Star.

My ego bigger than anyone can imagine. Even the dog's got a story going. Old dog, young child. Dog carries story of domesticated affection to next generation. I only feed the dog.

Environmentalist patent attorney for U. S. high technology corporation is coming to dinner. Fried potatoes, onions, Cornish hen stuffed with rice and mushrooms. Gravy from the beginning of time.

Pulse taken. The body stretched on stomach. Spine bare to rolling pressure of smooth forearm. Anglo-Russian Medical Dictionary to read tea leaves. Victims of heresy. Rublev. Massage. Wet with voyage. Clouds wet with voyage. Unusual rain. Hot tea after fatty meats dissolves grease in my intestines. Pulse, 62 over I don't know what. Feeling better but impatient. Can't wait any longer. Have to leave. Not getting any younger. Or growing more hair.

If there's energy enough to go back, there's enough energy to stay. I've landed. This civilizing. How about a moment's rest? Sleep aboard a ship under stars. No social obligations. Play with the dog. Get a job. Raise a family. Watch the family. Have a family.

Kayak. Kodiak. Ur-pop. Culturally behind. Gorbachev, a figment of history. History a figment. Ur-pop.

Michael's Great Potatoes! Borscht. Get a car, insurance. Ride around the block. Walk to the market. Buy a back scratch. Village on the shore, juts out of the fog into morning. Radiation. Population explosion. Immigration. Racism.

"That the Jews, not Washington, D. C., for a piece of good luck. It's not easy thing to be doctor of urology, living in Leningrad, or re-animator, on an ambulance," Leonid says. "Worst that could happen is to die. Inside nursery, also children, not just nurse, the plants, what does it mean? Doctor, please help."

8 a.m. Food Stamp case worker twenty minutes late. Fill out forms. Explain forms. Hand in forms. First in, last out. Lose motivation.

Hero. Good Father. Guide through driving tests. Three times and we get it right. Halfway there. The engine starts.

A cobweb lute.

Unwound. . .

Every minute, I feel mortality.

Any moment unconnected from morning light.

Dancing to my finger tapping on clipboard pad in San Mateo County Social Welfare Office.

High tones. High tones. Circuitry of plankton on reef. Seashells. Bromeliads. Listen to myself.

Urban cicada in rooms of California Transportation Dept. Cars parked in the driveway. Dreaded mechanic bills. Shopping list for family of five, formerly two. Instant teenagers.

Daylight Savings Time. Take inventory. Take inventory.

Mice get in the ship hold, deplete inventory. Then mold could form. Pesticides, a new theme factor in evolution.

Environmental movement.

Hallucination. Real buds open blue flowers.

En keloheinu, en keloheinu, Egypt for the Jew. I never knew I thought that way. Race is not a religion.

And all.

Chelated steppingstones mounting through snowflakes melt imagination, real morning light, several parallel voices off.

Parallel Voids.

I saw it on the table as we talked about Andrew Marvell, Adorno. Awkwardness of protest.

Inhuman Voids and humane reading of Eden. Redemption after Auschwitz. Humans forget sand beaches, bruised succulents, motion, cypress leaves, coping. . .

Trust myself, I have no choice.

I'd like to film Dagovich at Oberstein's Pesach dinner.

Huge flowing sawgrass river, flowing down a state.

Flowing animals and earth, river pulling down crocodiles, reed fish, oyster beds by falling tides, fiddler crabs in clatter across mounding mangrove muck, pulling hooks out of tangling tides, black in childhood fears.

"If some Jew, someday, wanted to take care for me, what's the shame?"

Look how it snags, juts, clacks.

Two Big Macs. One cheeseburger. Two large fries. Two fish sandwiches. Hot Fudge Sundae for Margarita. Soviet Union still exists, only Dagovich is changed.

Soot on Soviet streets. Carbon air.

Man, woman, child play in the lobby of Department of Motor Vehicles. Hopscotch on red arrow pointing to Line C: NEW LICENSES. How old are you? What's your name? Yes. NO. Black girl in thick braids.

Refund support.

Suspend the sails. The ship pulling.

Food Stamps approved. For a family of three to qualify for Food Stamps, they can't make more than $1,100 dollars per month income. Medical guaranteed for four months for refugees.

Fog like charcoal. Biggest mistake you can make is philosophic. Jane comes in.

"What did you see?" I ask her.

"I see many words, expressions, California, in number of colors. How many colors? Looks like a photograph. . ."

Later Leonid comes in my room to visit.

"In Soviet Union many Jews are wealthy. Everywhere they know to go to highest schools. Felix, he's very rich, buys four yachts at 40,000 rubles. It would take me a lifetime, without anything, to make 40,000 rubles. Maybe he has million rubles. He has everything he wants but afraid for his life. It's very dangerous to be a Jew with money now in Soviet Union. If they kill you, they say, because he was Jew."

"Arrive at midnight. SFO. Can't see the world, in the morning, first look out the window. Window frames the green hills, blue sky, seven colors of ocean, framed like postcards we saw from United States, California, Israel. In Soviet Union it was like the book, black and red. It was shock. And every day it's same."

"I don't know whether it's my mind, because it's new life, or good people I'm with, or it's really like that. Many colors. Memory of Byelorussia, places in Leningrad, when I was in Italy waiting to complete emigration, waiting for you to settle details with HIAS, while he was working out a contract for my life. My family not included in sponsorship. They will not be able to come to United States until I have enough money to sponsor them myself. By then my great-grandmother who is 92 will be dead, her mind bad because of age."

"You don't have to love your government or its bureaucracy to be patriotic. Patriotic can be for motherland. I think of Byelorussia. I have family there. They are very good people. Caseworker says, love of earth is not unusual amongst all Russian immigrant refugees she has met. Collecting mushrooms, their folk songs. Farmers. Peasants. Sit by road to Kanev, tin bucket of potatoes, laced sacks. The Soviets ashamed of them. They drink vodka, spend only money on today, no future. . .

Leonid has a big fat black moustache like Groucho Marx.

"Maybe I'm melodramatic, but there's a kink in every word that makes it okay. I want to be American. I want to sing patriotic songs, if I can sing without oppression."

Upbeat. . .

"I don't have to be rich. I think other maps have been charted. Maybe Oberstein will give medical insurance. It's very important to have health insurance. You don't just throw life away, future for children. Stuff your pockets with money, they will never be empty, until you can be sure of your future, for Margarita."

I remember at the Department of Motor Vehicles. A boy with a toy car was blocking Margarita from her game of hopscotch on broken red line. Margarita pushed the boy out of the way. And then they became friends. After Leonid and Jane get their car papers signed, and photograph for identification papers and driver's license. On the way out, the little boy knocked on the window, waved goodbye to Margarita.

"I'm taking over the lives of my family, not mine. I am also without reason. Crazy is unclear mind, working with senility at Oberstein's clinic."

Cut lamb from bone. Shashlik. Glass of asparagus tips on windowsill.

Idealist...

"Russia beautiful in very sick way. Pogroms. From mother to daughter, father to sons. All Jews know about, pogrom, means to do like thunder. Most Jews in Russia like 18th century bourgeoisie began in Russia, Germany. Germans killed many. Some are peasants, never farmers. 7th century law that Jew can't own land, work for farmers maybe. Everyone in hurry. Yes, for future."

"Very difficult to explain life in Soviet Union," he says, "to someone who hasn't been there. Don't know what it is to be Israeli soldier. Children throw rocks. Something wrong, Arab children carry guns like in Afghanistan."

"Pogroms. Hitler. Small Israel. Jew sends money from generation to generation to provide. Educated. There's no other way. How to live? Now to America. Occasionally swastika on bus, desecrate a temple. One of two Jews in Daly City, was different. Simchas Torah is fun. Eat nuts and honey. Sweet New Year. Rosh Hoshana. Honey and apples. We can afford to buy apples. Organic apples cost too much but this is not anti-semitism."

"I maybe want to be physician. Not like Oberstein, too many old people. It's very difficult, all day drawing blood. I laugh, they laugh, we laugh about nothing. It's crazy, old people. Not only senility, but crazy, mind unclear. They laugh for no reason. I am also without reason. Physician is good but it's better to talk, take time."

"They stand around me. Yevgenya and Margarita. Margarita has backpack for school. Yevgenya, a driver's lesson from Nancy. Nancy, and a glass of champagne, Michael with decisions to explain. It's good. It's great!"

"*Who Framed Roger Rabbit?*" Popcorn. Night, we sleep. Saturday. Easter Weekend. *Sesame Street.*

In Soviet Union, celebration everyone goes to restaurant.

Leonid, you will fit well, your middle-class habits prepare you for travel, assimilation. Who is this family? They aren't mine. Who are these people, these Jews? Who gives privileges?

"The second thing, surprise, in United States is people. When we came into American airplane, we saw stewardess. They had great smile through all their faces. All Soviet immigrants was hesitated what they can do, whether to smile or put their face to ground. It's big difference between not only Soviet Union, but in Italy. In spite it being a very sunny place, not so ugly faces like Soviet faces. They are more smiley, have friendly faces, their behavior more friendly. The first time, and now also, when we went with Margarita up the hill, when I went to work, and from work, all people saying hi and hello. Margaret asked me, I don't know these people, why they tell me hi or hello? I try to tell her it's usually thing in United States."

"Why didn't you go to Israel? Your mother and father, your sister, live in Israel?" I ask.

"When we were in Uzbekistan, I saw level of medicine. It's under bottom, lower than Soviet Union. I thought, all Jewish people have great money in Uzbekistan. I never see how they work. All time they have holiday. When circumcision, when they have new house, when the Jewish man died. Every week, whole week from his death, whole week people celebrate seven weeks, months, all people drink, pray, discuss. As result, every day they have holiday, have brandy. Life not so hard."

"All Uzbekistan Jews are coming to Moscow and Leningrad to treat their sick. In Uzbekistan doctors buy diploma. When Saturday, the old woman comes to your house, every house has a big yard with chairs and big tables. They say, to the old woman, you are washing or working on Saturday. I cannot be free man if other people saying what I am doing in my own yard. I'm afraid if you live in Israel you live like Uzbekistan. And Israel medicine, it's easier to be doctor in Israel than United States. It's not good work. People are saying the level is good, but it's not good work. And Israel, so many people from Soviet Union, it becomes like Soviet Union. Not Soviet, but union. Happiness for my children is happiness."

$756.00 per month for four months guarantees sponsorship of refugee family. Secondary Family Agreement, supports all secondary family that may wish to emigrate to U.S. for next six months. Bills come daily. Overdue notices from Dutch suppliers. Can't talk about this to Dagovich. What difference would it make? They couldn't eat less. He makes $720.00 a month. She doesn't work. It wouldn't be any cheaper if they left. If I had more time, I couldn't make more money. We're all working.

America loves a nightmare. Rice is boiling over. The smoke alarm mimics hysteria. Dog eye's glazed from stroke. Stroked to death.

Another English lesson eleven o'clock in kitchen, sorting through appointments, vaccination for the child.

There for the grace of god goes the bell that tolls. Arm aching with anticipation. Slug me. Whole body tense with gastritis. Angels tap my sternum. Deer with antlers pronging from shoulders. Bearded doe carouses without confined love. Set the tribe running from garden into thundering fires of Cossacks. Scourge of typhus. Scapegoats.

Got to have wheels. Got to buy car. Get insurance. Make sure I don't speed and it doesn't break down.

The diaspora. When we were in the temple. . .

Are all answers to questions asked by Social Welfare Bureau true?

Leonid returns.

"It's very difficult without language to send a letter. That's truth. In one hand, it's good my family will be born in United States. It's true you weren't born in the United States, but on the other hand, it's very good for me and Jane and Margarita that we see Soviet reality, and after that can see American reality."

"The best land to be born in is United States. Twelve in cards is unreal. I think that what it looks like when someone all his life lives on best conditions, he has the best food, has the best car, the best house, all the best, and when he was on the end of life's way. It looks like the Soviet doctor polyclinic, ambulatory, when doctor never takes patient in his house, he only sees the faces of people, like Oberstein, people sometimes take their clothes away. That's not a good comparison. Like the man who is working on the seacoast where is the flash, lighthouse, he never sees the other, only sea, coast birds, and I told it that maybe the best have many kind of comparisons, to have compare between bad thing and good thing, not so bad and the best, to have difference between things, for example Soviet life, American life, American car, Soviet car, Leningrad weather, California weather."

"I think it is the best thing to travel. Every time, have new picture, new things, new food, and this man compares his life, if he has his health. I think so it's good, when you can compare with other things, when you all have the same thing, good quality, bad quality, variety. It's not necessary to travel to have emotions because every day we don't travel there is still a lot of emotions."

The U. S. welfare system is a good system if you have money. The person wakes up from the dream, drives to work in his own car, forty-five minutes there, thirty minutes back. Lunch. Drive-up McDonald's. Bring lunch back to the Oberstein's office, eat at the big table.

We trade plants for a car.

Another blessing from whatever is destiny.

Mazda 626, 4 door, gold-brown paint with dark brown trunk. It wouldn't open, so they had to get a new trunk, but got the wrong color. Maybe it was rear ended. No, it was a good used car. Asked $1200 dollars. We took it to a mechanic who said it was fine, worth $800.00. The engine is running.

We got driver's license. The brake lights wouldn't work, wouldn't let him take test. Took off work for this. Please DMV, let us run, get it fixed, come back, take the test. Okay? We ran over to Shell station down the street, opened the trunk, fixed the loose bulb. The mechanic helped us for free! I locked the keys in the trunk. The mechanic tried to pry the trunk open. Leonid found the hole in the back seat for the snow skies to go through. Thank the Swedes for knowing how to build a car. Leonid stuck his hand through the ski hole, and fished in trunk darkness. He found the keys.

We rushed back, took the test. Leonid passed. Drove to Millbrae, Richard Murphy Insurance, got insurance. Dick told him the ins and outs, explained coverage, the law, tickets, and enjoyed it totally, helping the immigrant make it in the New World.

We drove insured in Leonid's car to DMV, Daly City, register the car we traded for plants. We can't register because car needs a smog device. This isn't meant to be funny.

The clerk named Pushkin, behind the counter at DMV, knew nyet and da, going to Leningrad to visit soon. Her family in the US for many generations. She was pissed at Leonid, that an immigrant could get a car so fast, when it took her 20 years saving up money and help from her parents before she could afford a car herself. She said it would take 20 minutes for smog certificate down the street.

"Here." Pushkin says, "A day pass. Come back and I'll register it."

Sitting in the car, talking about women, the mechanic passes the car, gives us a smog certificate. We run back to DMV, it's 5:00 p.m. It closes at five o'clock. I ask him please, Mr. DMV, let me in, I have this pass, it will only take a minute. That's about all it took. Inside, Pushkin gave us the registration. We drove home. It was time to take Jane to Mission St., Jefferson High to take an English test.

Job Club for Jane.

Leonid and I are going to Slim's to see Marianne Faithfull and Barry Reynolds. Leonid in dark blue, pin stripe suit, casually cool.

Michael Heller, a poet from New York comes to visit.

"Did you know that I teach and administer a large English as a Second Language operation at NYU? Some of the problems you describe with your Russian émigrés, I see on a daily basis. Not only 'culture shock' but the carloads of cynicism, the Russians in particular, have imported into just about every sphere of their new American lives. In academia, already a bureaucracy, full of forms, mass anonymities, and inscrutable requirements, their (the Russians) underlying suspicions and anxieties soar into full bloom. Any official looking piece of paper is an arrest warrant or an extortion or hoodwink. Yes, the transitions are interesting."

2

It's an age of disbelief. Lithuania wants independence. Moscow cuts the gas off. Fortunately, it's Spring. Margarita gets a vaccination. Two shots in one arm, one shot in the other. They wouldn't give her vaccinations in the leg, as my mother suggested, as her mother did for her, so the scar would be less visible when wearing a strapless gown. Jane said it's just as unpleasant on the leg. Everything changing. Tension in my back is the headache of confession. A plane passing overhead sounds like thunder. 64 tremors and a woman is leaning against a wall screaming. It's a trade-off. Who is being heard the least?

Bob Brown from an investment firm in San Marino wants to know what I know about the convention center Mr. Sette is trying to build on Mori Point, funded by a surgeon and a dentist with a combined net worth of thirty million dollars. The project is trying to raise eight million dollars in financing. Bob's too conservative and environmental to get involved, although they're offering him five points. Low financing. They're going to buy Sette out for 5% of the offering.

He's out of the deal. The dentist is an idiot. Bob said every dentist he's known is an idiot. I told Bob I wouldn't let them build the project. It'll never get built. I've got to call Hal, find out what we should do.

Wipe yourself with this pad, a few drops in the toilet, the rest in the cup.

The Vietnamese woman jabbed me with her elbow.

Dagovich. . .

Up until five in the morning watching T.V.

"I'm empty not tired. The T.V. took my blood, took my full. I'm like foolish man without idea in mind, because I have a good relax. The great relax is no idea in mind. Maybe because of next week, I have no appointment. I'm more tired to wait without steps. I like the puppet of Shakespeare on the shelf."

"Thinking when Oberstein will give me more money, if he has idea about it in mind. Thinking about washing car process, to wash and clean inside, it's good feeling. Better than to think about next appointment. It's not so difficult to think about lower level, when you have idea about car for your mind, it is rest. Vegetable thoughts. Clean first the motor. Control liquids in car, not liquids in my body."

"What is this in the cup, in the gas, water, coffee? To fill. I can sit now, tell I'm very glad to see picture in the window because outside the window are house, are babies crying, is not my mind. It's very simple to take words from your mouth, to say it's the wall without trees. It's not true what's in your mind, if you have other thing in your mind, going to another appointment. It's not the same thing as if you see the wall. There's a difference between imagination and imagination. There are many kinds. It's not imagination if you see wall, and see trees. It's not true. It's way to give empty cup full.

"To take. It's like stretching time. If you see wall you need to tell about, or if you seen wall to fill time fifteen minutes. In our case it looks like we stretch time to talk about tree we can't see on this wall. It's not good to fill your life with idea about clean wall, without wall, without pictures, it's better to have black wall."

Work on the bed. On the book. On the car. Work on the washing. In the male. I know, you don't understand."

Yes, I understand they buried the eel.

Snowflake in the yard.

The child sucks a lollipop, got underfoot, feeding hand in the Dagwood tradition. The bed being made.

Alex has got viral pneumonia, comes at a shitty time, when he's supposed to be making ten thousand dollars a week, filing immigration papers. Three hundred dollars a head.

Nancy's determined to make a book.

Dagovich washing a car with the radio on outside on Saturday morning. Overcast coastal Saturday morning. Get up with rest of weekly Americans. Watching movies until five in the morning. Waking empty.

Empty mind, best mind. No thoughts. No appointments. First week no mind.

Check in with friends, neglected projects, shop operations. Chicken sandwich in the kitchen with Nancy.

Earth Day, 1990. Recycle.

McDonald's wants to spend $100,000,00 dollars on recycled materials.

What's your address? If you get lost, where's the policeman?

Steaks. Lamb chops. Tater Tots. Movie from another paradise. Eric Clapton, Elton John, George Harrison and Ringo Starr. Where's Dagovich? With daughter and wife? Chauvinist to Ben Franklin Store to buy shoes for child. She begins school on Monday. Tomorrow, she goes at 8:30 a.m. to Jewish Sunday School. Reformed convention.

Oberstein calls to see if Leonid wants to go to temple, why it would be good for Margarita on Sundays. She'll be going to camp with same kids this summer. As for Jane, who I am accused by Nancy of consigning to a typical female role, in the house without a career. I only suggested, she wanted to stay home because she said she wanted to stay home. She didn't want to send Margarita to childcare. I never recommended this, but wouldn't it be better for a mother to be with child if family could afford it? Wouldn't I stay home, raise the child, if I could afford it, rather than crawling all over America, paying 20% to taxes, bosses, buses, badminton and bones? When I could be sitting at home, writing, going out when I wanted to, if I had a car? But of course, my career is at home. Jane might not have a career, without working for somebody.

I think I'll call Ellen, see how her biopsy went.

Everyone out for Earth Day. Fog. Drizzly earth day. Walk on Mori Point with Hal. Lay down in wildflowers. Look over ocean, Pacifica beaches, marshland. Think about seven-story conference center on prominent ridgeline. Walk over concrete remains of Mori Point Inn. Burnt down. Years ago. Where you went without your wife. You had a great time. Remains of concrete and bar above isolate cove. Remains of buckshot shells, tin cans. Earth torn from dirt bike. 4-wheel, Ram-tough Joes looking over the beginning of another great American suburban poltergeist. Big, beautiful house with white picket fence, or hacienda, or California style.

Make a long story short. It was a human story once and for all. I woke for Yom Kippur.

Jonah, Sisyphus or Prometheus. Any perfect existential cloud.

Earth Day a la McDonald's. At Century 21 Realty: Every day is Earth Day. Leonid, Margarita and Jane take off for temple a la Oberstein. 8:30 a.m. on a holiday Sunday morning. It should have been Yom Kippur. Lights out. Pockets empty. Heater off. Stereo off. If you can't turn it off, if it's been on, then leave it on. Don't affect energy. Give the earth a rest. Every nonsense and good deed becomes a sermon, every sermon is unnecessary, every day is Earth Day, if you're human.

Dagovich and family in Mazda, shines from sponge rub. Sunday afternoon looking at ducks and bison in Golden Gate Park. Monday morning Sharp Park School. Margarita begins in acid jeans, cowboy boots. A bit of blue Russian lace, blue lace headband in her enormously long black hair.

What's to be done?

Margarita went to school. Taking the bus wasn't a problem for Jane. Only problem was the bus never came. Margarita made a friend, Tina. All the children said, Hi,

Margarita! A little boy with red spots on his face, freckles, red hair and hat. Hi, Margarita.

I say goodbye to New College friends in Chinese Restaurant. Tom Clark will teach us what we want to be taught, the way he wants to teach it. He says, Alice Walker, a farce as poet, besides *The Color Purple*. Frank O'Hara may be a gossip, but didn't invent gossip. Other modern phenomena, like Ntozake Shange. He asks, "Is it our responsibility to make up for iniquities of the past?" He asks, "Who were the giants? Crane? Stevens?" He taught who was giant for Richard Wilbur and the like: *Summer Knowledge* by Delmore Schwartz.

I'm talking to myself.

I'm going to call Ellen and see how she's doing. . .

She's home.

"Can you hold on a sec?"

"Hello. What's going on?"

"I got accepted by Yaddo."

Weren't we talking about death? Sloan Kettering Hospital harder to get into than Yaddo.

How a family understands Cancer. Mother had cancer. Some cancer attaches, like a growth. You cut it out. Isolated. Others spread through lymph system. Some, secondary, are hard to find. Some circulatory. Some treatable with chemotherapy. Some fatal. Some afraid to ask. Examine. Ask for a second opinion. Ellen's mother died from cancer. Now Ellen tells her children she has cancer, but she's not sick. Sick as in a cold. As in 100,000 dying in hospitals. Screaming against the wall, stinking as they're dying. Piled upon each other. Some are afraid. Family: You can't live with them, you can't kill them. They need consolation. Friends need consolation. You are dying. You must console the survivor. You will have forgotten the irregular breathing, gasp of your mother in her last living bed, early L.A. morning. Or father on the floor in Miami condominium, after another effort at feeling his life.

Discount school lunch for children on food stamps.

Daddy Dagovich calls home every afternoon from work to see how his wonderful daughter is doing, and the mother, Jane refuses to take money for helping us. Bookkeeping. We pick up Margarita at 1:35 p.m. We ask what she did today. She could understand. Her teacher was "hungry" or "angry." What she didn't understand, the children tried to explain. She ate a hot dog with ketchup, bread and milk. Heard record about Red Riding Hood, chickens and an animal she could only describe in Russian. Everyday it's easier and harder.

We watch the dog heal from his stroke. He can't climb but he can walk. My mother alone in Miami. She's going to a two hundred dollar a ticket concert. The ticket was a gift. "I wouldn't pay that much to watch Pavarotti eat." Her maid quit.

At the end of this week, I want to go to Tahoe, stay in a cabin. I want to gamble. I want to get stoned, drive around the lake. I want to go on into Nevada, New Mexico, Mexico, sit in a hollow boulder, look at clouds move, the sky, watch a campesino ride by, snake rattle dangling from hide strap, tied to the saddle horn. I want to be tortured by robbers who think I'm a DEA agent.

Can I do this for the rest of my life? Am I in such a hurry to be Dagovich? A country between mountains. Snow-capped and soaking my feet in Asia. Byelorussia. What about independence of Byelorussia? How about another Jewish state in the middle of Russia?

Hello, Daddy Dagovich. How are your Russians today? Chernobyl. Hot spots. Nuclear-active clouds drift over Byelorussia. Twisted yellow flowers. Pollen-less clouds deforming over the Ukraine. How are your Russians? How are your Vietnamese? How are you going to survive in Cambodia? La Fontaine stabbed in the throat by a woman carrying a bouquet of flowers. Pulls a long knife out of the bouquet. Could I have your autograph?

Perversion of bars in the puzzle of dreams. In the playground. In critical condition because I never learned to speak right. Chernobyl. Become a doctor. Modern medicine only a Bering Strait of ice water. Make the bed. Exercise, as if your life depended on it.

And if I can't ask you, I shouldn't be writing. You know how afraid he is of historical Russian. Huge, histrionic, big-booked Russians. Big-hearted, social-minded blubbering belligerent, sable-hatted pogromista, and Peter the Great who had a hobby of pulling teeth.

Elizabethan knot gardens. Circadian rhythm that makes you sap, drowse, sap, drowse. Biological clocks, "the habits of 46 'fluctuating' flowers. Grouped into three categories. Meteoric, in response to atmosphere, tropical, according to day length, equinoctial, stuck to their internal guns, opening and closing at regular times, relatively oblivious to external acts of nature. Using plants of the last class, Linnaeus, at the age of fifteen, designed the first true flower clock. He referred to it as *horologium plantarum*. Apparently, it was a collection of potted plants arranged on his desk."

Rehabilitation Through Training. Kaplan School. M.D. Oberstein lends Jane a red dress. Thoughtful though she prefers blue. Naomi from Jewish Vocational Service.

Mole in United States government feeds me secrets on workings of EPA. Midnight calls from Leningrad. Leonid. Jane. Margarita. It's confidence not genius, that's the spirit of household.

Clear weather all week.

"At thirty I want to be doctor again. In Italy, I was the only one who worked."

9:00 a.m., Terrence and Karen open Golden Gate Park Conservatory Shop. Cash box gone but the register tapes remain. Whodunit? No forced entry. Five employees have cabinet keys. Five employees have keys to the building. And there's a padlock to the gazebo. Someone had to have a key to the gazebo padlock. Someone had to have a key to the building, the padlock, the cabinet.

Talking to Hal about Mori Point lawsuit, Sette trying to get investors, sends out prospectus, claims he's got permits for houses, doesn't mention a lawsuit. Talking to Hal about SEC, environmental stuff and how hard it is to make $50.

Then Terrence calls, says a thousand dollars is missing. It could be the security guard, always hanging around, watching them count up daily receipts. Or the janitor with something loose in his head. Try to talk to him. Or Margret, she's got an attitude problem. Karen's defensive. Terrence stutters. Everyone wears reflective glasses, even the cop who took the robbery report. Admission money stolen. City of San Francisco money. Money from coffee mug and postcard sales.

Olga explains Medical exam to Leonid, Kaplan intensive course for foreign medical students. How to study? How to work? How to eat? speak?

Marliss thinks it's the Janitor. He came early, left for an hour, then came back. Margret thinks it's the security guard who closed up at 6:40 p.m., because one day he asked her what kind of padlock we use.

"We have bad events today." Stretched out on floor. Yawn. "Today we had two shocks. About myself. The first was the material what Olga gave me. It's awful thing. It's terrible. It's new system of education, maybe. New words. I expected it will be many same words what Latin language and English medical language. No, it's not true. English medicine has some names. Street language. Same languages people they are using when they are speaking their neighbors, friends, dogs and cats. It's good for my English language because it's the same words. But it's not so good for my medical studying because there are a lot of new words. Too much for beginning. Maybe good for beginning. And the second bad news was the story about Gift Shop. But, second story I hope will have good end, a happy end. We must do something to have happy end. Maybe study. Maybe looking for what else. Your brother Bruce tomorrow has birthday. Official. It's better for Bruce to have birthday on 29th than 28th because today is not happy day. It's usual thing in Soviet Union when someone steals money, in other things."

"In Soviet Union, it's impossible to live only with money you have from your payment. My payment only 200 rubles. Food only cost 210 rubles minimum. Many people that has 100 rubles, especially engineers or scientist workers. It's very big problem in Soviet Union to have money. I saw it many times. People steal many things, especially from state. Like people after work taking wood from factory to their cars and home. In factory, someone working on the radio, it's usual thing to steal them, a lot of details."

"Black market. For example, in my work a lot of people steal alcohol because it is expensive in Soviet Union to have vodka from shop. Without paying they can take alcohol. There are a lot of recipes for making good things from alcohol. All medical personnel took from their homes materials for bandage, cotton, any you like, all that is possible, apparatus for blood pressure. Every day from my work was morning conference of doctors, nurses. Someone steal one less blood pressure instrument. We have one less."

"There are many methods to liquidate. For example, in paper you have thirty apparatus. At end of month, you can put that five more are broken. Maybe because of it I was surprised that someone steal from gift shop. It's very easy to steal from shops. For example, you stay your car without lock, it's unreal thing in Soviet Union. It's guarantee you next day radio or glasses are gone. Lemon peel in alcohol during one week, to mix with mineral water, it will be very good taste. Like lemon vodka, it's very clear because it's without oils, only lemon oils. Best thing is to do it with green grass, menthol taste, mint. Put in bottle with alcohol. Spiritus. 96% alcohol in medicine is usually. Spiritus Vine. Not rubbing alcohol but medical alcohol. I didn't use this thing. I could buy vodka, if I need it, in the shop. I worked like taxi. It's possible to have fifty rubles during one day. It's very hard work especially after work."

"One thing I steal all the time from work was gas. For ambulance. It's state gas. Everyone drive of ambulance has little paper with sign says twenty liters. Like seven gallons super gas. Ok, I had a lot of friends who are drivers of state machines. They gave me papers for gas, then every night I with my friends who work with me in ambulance, come to me with friends who work at the gas station. I took twenty-liter canister. It was good for me. It was like 40 kopeks for liter. 16 rubles to fill tank. Impossible to have car without stealing gas. Maybe it wasn't necessary, but it was very interesting."

"I like to go to the gas station. There was very pretty women at gas station. It was rest period for me. They drink coffee. You could sleep in ambulance in special bed, rest your health. All people with who I worked liked this one. It really helped for my budget, because, okay, it was 160 rubles to my pocket every month in gas, every three to six days. Ambulance driver and nurse, they liked it because it was rest for them. Ambulance driver, every time he take the gas from ambulance car. It's the system of Soviet society. Everybody, every time, everyone has something from their work. It's usual thing. It's illegal."

"There's humor about it. For example, one woman came to the temple, talked to the rabbi, 'I want to marry my daughter off. Do you have someone for my daughter?' 'Yes,' he tells her, he has a lot of them for her. She says, 'What kind of men? What are they?' She was interested what they are. Rabbi says, 'I have one, he is great violinist. He's got twice high Leningrad education, Moscow and Leningrad Conservatory education. I have one engineer. I don't know what kind of man you want.' She says, 'I don't know, maybe you have a butcher.' Because all butcher in Soviet Union are like butcher in United States. More than gas by a thousand time. When someone comes to shop, the state inspector has from this kind of man maybe one-thousand-dollar payoff to say everything is okay. It's normal thing for all Soviet society."

"It's unreal thing to live only for your payment. If you are very honest, you can't live in Soviet Union because it's death. It's very bad thing, especially for children, because they are seeing what parents are doing. They hear about this. It's very bad thing for raising children. It's not so hard for yourself to do this operation with gas. I's like game. It's like rest time for your mind and health. Other direction for your mind. Other direction for ambulance driver. Maybe if all people stopped this bad deals maybe Soviet Union be great country."

Everyone joins the parade. Red-flagged river flows into Red Square. Gorbachev on TV Lithuania and Soviet Union working out a compromise to independence, although one says independence is not negotiable, and the other says we will not negotiate with separatists, says they are not following rules. Soviet Union cuts power to Lithuania. Lithuania embarrasses everyone who was saying what good Gorbachev is doing. Leonid saying Gorbachev is a product of the times. He is willing to work within the dictates and constraints of history. Gorbachev another fad. Hugging babies in Europe.

Under socialist sun, utopian fire. Chernyshevsky with a sense of humor pilfering a woodpile at furniture factory. Fringe benefits in beneficial state. Theft without motion. Stealing a thousand dollars from me. It's still there, in a closet at home, next to a telltale heart and eraser dust. It was my money.

"I told her a hundred times, don't feed the dog. This is parenthood. Two women stand over a child. The dog is panting. Yo-yo. I used yo-yo. My father used yo-yo. Every American ought to use yo-yos."

Lichens. Pine needles.

Three deer on rutted road on the hill. Looking at us.

"Margarita wants so much to see them. Vodka says to sleep."

Olives, Prosciutto. Champagne. Seafood Shashlik.

Bruce's Birthday. Black Ruben, the Briard, barks through sunroof of "Brehz's" black Italian sports car on Sunday afternoon.

Hal windsurfs in San Francisco Bay. Nancy teaches self-defense against rape. Margarita puts toys together in the yard. Bandit's locked up because of hostility towards Ruben.

May Day in Red Square. Protesters in Kremlin. 100-year anniversary. Food is not luxury. Ukrainian independence movement, one more time. Lithuanian, Azerbaijani, Rumanian, all voices slow joining in response. Latvia. Estonia. Vera Pavlova. Verochka's good at running a seamstress shop. Galina says Vera would eat anything with cream in it to get at the cream. Utopians vote for Democrats to get at cream. More important, Margarita got invited to a birthday party on Saturday at 1:30 p.m., RSVP. Margarita doesn't know what the invitation says. Or whose party it is. Or who Batman is. It's a Batman birthday card. I don't know what they're getting at. People want to eat, buy stereos, discover society, the universe.

May Day in Red Square.

Plans add up to know plans, run out the door. This is the right place to be. Finger bandaged. Tried to spear an avocado pit. What is this slippery excitement? Someone in the family has got to make a living.

Why did I marry a shiksa? I thought I was rich.

Brother signs up for unemployment.

Jane's doing the right thing. Studies bookkeeping at Shelldance. Takes English school at night. No place in America for a food engineer, when HUD has been pilfering the taxpayer's money, Reagan deregulated all the industries so that industrialists can take a profit. Intelligentsia reading Chernyshesky and making jokes about Mayakovsky in the garden.

Re-dreaming ancient texts then walking outside into the garden. Teach English to immigrants who are skeptical about systems. Ronald Reagan can't remember the day before George Bush took over. Suddenly senile he rides his horse, pats his dog.

Clam sauce pilfers the air.

Da. Da. Da.

Margarita had to buy a gift for the boy who's having a birthday party on Sunday afternoon. His mother says he likes Batman and baseball cards. I think of yo-yos. And this is where I'm supposed to tell you what I've been thinking about for the last five weeks. We got a food stamp check today.

Market St., a homeless hangout. Dealers and dopers. Osiris and Persephone popping Quetzacoatl in tiny vials, balls on the great Mayan playing fields are flying endlessly, atoms resonating off a grab in my eye.

The greenhouse is hot. It's time to take offsets, divide and secure for the summer. Preparing for a foliar explosion, but it's not happening, and I need a vacation. Also, about thirty thousand dollars. Would last me another five years. I can live economically and do what I like to do. Drink diet Pepsi. Drop into the comic store and blow two dollars and eighty-eight cents on a Batman comic, the newest. I asked the man if it just came out today. Two packs of Batman cards with gum. A Batman button. "It's my job." Someone's got to do it.

I cook spaghetti. Make everyone dinner.

3

Remove the bandage from my finger. Leonid's gone to take Jane to School. Nancy's in the kitchen washing spaghetti pots and pans. Margarita watches *He-Man*.

I haven't thought of anything too intellectual since I got off the plane.

Courting disaster, becoming a tree when I could have become a Russian Jewish Refugee from Leningrad. Collect food stamps while I work as lab technician in San Mateo Medical Clinic. Taking blood and urine tests all day, while John Keats buzzes about immortality and negative capability. Or I could be me, find a pace, ride a car.

Pogrom. Pogrom.

Batman.

Pure encasement.

Passive word, to receive, rather than the more active, to get.

Outside schoolroom at 1:35 p.m. The kid hasn't learned a new word though she waits for explosion in which language is nothing to learn but to be played with.

Memory and all songs that came before.

What language do you speak?

Me, I speak Russian. I don't know. What language do you speak?

I speak English.

If you're going to live here, you ought to speak English. If you don't, and have problems, and you complain to me, forget it. I've got no sympathy.

What language do you speak?

I speak English.

In this country, if you want to have an opportunity you have to speak at least English. Let it pass through you. Get up in the morning, theory of leather and fraud, the popular myth is Milliken. The Hunt brothers. Financial scum trying to be Hannibal.

The imagination of the frog man is proportionate to his will to die. Dwarf in a sloshing sea of porpoise poop. Carnival. If I could look at trees and write about them at the same time I would be a schizophrenic or a genius. But I'm not the hero.

Punk Rockwell.

Publish. Edit. Provide a translation of Leon Duval's 1896 French handbook on bromeliad culture.

Merchandise it.

Punk Rockwell.

Vomits Russia. Cabbage, lamb and rice.

Punk Rockwell. Punk.

Vomits Russia. Lumps of words. Classics resurrected in prose poetry, in politics, as if it were different than religion.

Amorous dark smile of Tajik haremette.

I've got a headache. I want to get it out of mind.

Punk Rockwellian.

Get a doctor to be a nurse. Get a child to talk.

Dark-eyed blinking, nervous twitch.

School. School. I feel like demanding they stay here so they can understand. What difference does it make, they have their own life. Old enough to know American Reality. Headache. American, Soviet Reality.

One hundred pages of reality. Orchids in mail to mother. Someone else's life not at my disposal. If I ask you for twenty minutes to come into my room to talk to me, tell me about your life.

I think it's an image to live with.

They're going to take a walk up the hill. I'm invited if I want. But that's not what I want. I want Leonid to come sit with me by my computer. Talk with me, tell me about his life so I can tell my friends what it's like to house a Soviet Jewish refugee family named Dagovich from Leningrad. Call me at my home, ask me what it's like to live with someone you don't even know. Next thing we know you'll adopt an exchange student!

I am going to publish a book on Bromeliads. The Bromeliad Society has come up with support money, and a book dealer in the Netherlands is taking 150 copies in advance. It would be sweet to run a foundation. Publish books and art, never worry about cost. Forever.

The phone rings.

PUNK ROCKWELL'S NIGHTMARE OF THE VIOLIN

At the river with a bucket, dip it in the water
pieces of a dream float by. . .
A man sleeping
A bum sits on a bed, whispers

First story is about Fat Lady.
He gets picked up by this big woman & she swallows him.
The story takes place inside of her

She sneezes him out ~
The bum keeps coming in room
He wakes

You must dream
Why does he have dreams?
His kingdom to conquer
The Kingdom of his dreams lives inside of him
Dream characters send bum to his brain
tell him to keep dreaming because
he keeps them from fading, keeps them alive
Among those funny dreams he's got to save. . .
Meets brooding snakes, pouting since the Fall
Good Snakes are his army
Creatures of No-Dreams are his enemies
Bankers & car mechanics are
in the army of the creature of No-Dreams
He falls in love with a Harem of Women 1
Not just one

Who is the sympathetic character of dreams?

Black
White
Black
White glint

Green Road
Falling Yellow green Roar Farm equipment
Organic Farmer
Day Fears are how to get a crop without chemicals.
His hopes are to get crops to market.
He talks to a dog about their crop.
They both work the farm.

Rockwell – Character
Dog's Name is Punk

Big Lady Gets him – swallows him
Falls in Belly of a Woman

THUD

4

Time is beginning to come apart.

40 years old writing under the shadow of a four-thousand-year-old *sequoiadendron*.

Eating mushrooms. Watching ink flicker dry on the page. Smoke from the rustic cabin chimney. Fly on my hand. Taste a little. Ink leaks from the pen. Black on my hand. This sort of thing hasn't happened in years. I'll go wash.

Nancy coming down the road from the hotel communal toilet, abhors my yellow legal pad. These pads were all over my house.

"There's a picnic table, Michael. Want a bite of apple?" she asks.

Zoom. Zoom. Chirp. Caw.

Earl of Leicester seduced in a rowboat on the Thames by a Victorian amazon. Caw. Caw. Sun on my limbs takes the night chill out. It's May! Ants, flies, zoom, crawl in pine straw, sticks, bark flakes. Green lichen bits. Building it.

That's what I said, sitting on the ground outside of the cabin.

Lucasfilm. Hanson Muppets. Nightmare Baseball cards.

Foot model.

Her feet are perfect. Nancy can be a foot model.

The less thoughts I have, the less incarnations.

THE LESS THOUGHTS I HAVE, THE LESS INCARNATIONS.

Bergeri, tenuifolia, geminiflora.

Make dibble-board. Make dibble-board.

Contact Maarschalk about *tectorum*, cut flowers. Send *tectorum* to Ruth Owades.

What products are now occupying the shelves like glass and crystal were? Get them.

Ask Paul's Press about Coke machine. Car mechanics and bankers screwing country ever since Ronald Reagan deregulated everything and gave them permission.

Satire on fucking car mechanics. Dildo idiot car mechanics smart enough to know you need your car. I should start a garage. Hire car mechanics.

10' 6".

They'll need a union to protect them.

Don't ask anybody for help. The news. Read the news!

Television news special about bombing of Pan Am passenger jet over Scotland. Some people want to blame Pan Am. Others want to blame Iran and Saudi Arabia. An international terrorist scandal in which the civilized world can't police itself. Nearly the entire world is civilized.

10' 6", Punk Rockwell enters a time machine, time falling apart, leaving his body on the shower stall floor.

By their nature, defense mechanisms have to be perfect otherwise you die. In John Donne's "The Anniversaries," "Progress of the Soul." By not nearly mentioning the nausea, but living the memory over again, afraid, at any minute, history will swallow me up, spit me out whole. Another progress of a soul.

Archaeology of an age in Donne's "Anniversary." Hostile to Women. Prisoners of their times and the times have not changed.

Who died and made you god?

Punk Rockwell trying to think of the next thing to think, and not think so much that he doesn't know how he got home.

Was it nothing? Does it matter. Stones. Water. Snakes.

Who died and made you god?

Who died?

The asshole in the streetcar is a poet. He teaches at a girl's school, tells children he despises how they should live their lives. Running away from anyone who might question his mind, open his mind. Same asshole who twenty years earlier taught me to open my mind.

Who died and made you god?

Who drove you down from Sierra sequoia trees? Yellow flowers. Fremontia and lupine. On the road that took me down out of the mountains.

Why did you die?

It was inevitable.

Rolling on the bed, I want to forget the muscular Pocahontas with Swedish eyes, the steam in the shower and the drug.

I died and made you god.

You died and made yourself god.

I'm dead. I'm god.

Punk Rockwell, 10' 6", aid to Russian refugees, bromeliad grower, trader of Nightmare Baseball Cards.

Punk Rockwell, businessman in a bamboo hut in the Silicon chip age, Information age, Administration age, Environmental age.

Romantic Punk looks down upon the sequoias, watches his body decay.

He must come down before he catches a chill.

I look at her, she's holding me up.

I'm coming. She thinks I mean I'm coming. But I mean I'm coming back to my body. The steam of the shower and the altitude of the mountains. I think I'm going to faint.

Apparently, I did.

Punk Rockwell took sides, went to Leningrad, met a Russian Doctor Dagovich and his family, nearly dropped dead making them a new life in America.

Daddy Dagovich saying he didn't think it was such a good idea. "I think us here is not good for you."

People ask how my Russians are. Which is sort of like saying, "How are your children?" So, I tell Dagovich if you can't be my hero at least learn how to speak English. I don't think the Soviet system is fair. I don't think the Soviets have a system.

But he's born again!

He did that already in his previous human story.

What's the difference?

Well, in the first human story, before the Fall, Punk Rockwell just dies for no reason, then un-dies because he realizes he has no choice.

Proud jerking of the shrine. Lyric muse tugs at my breast.

Detoxification. Re-hydration. Water by my bed. Nancy stokes the fire.

There was that moment without breath.

She saw me stop breathing, unconscious.

She lowered me down to the bench and waited.

What a waste, a naked man my age with a silly drug. I came back to my body because I was too embarrassed to die this way.

I told her to lead me to the cabin, but don't touch me.

I walked down the asphalt path through the sequoias, towel over my neck, my hair wet. I felt like shaman, an initiate. I couldn't see the sequoias, but I knew they were there.

She walked ahead of me.

Initiated, I walked to the cabin and laid in bed.

In the shower, I was afraid, over and over again. I leaped for my breath. I took a deep breath and groaned myself back again.

I laid down in bed.

Nancy covered me with blankets and gave me water. She gave me strawberry papaya nectar. Lit incense.

"There you go. Doesn't that taste good?" she said.

It was her way of welcoming me back.

Acknowledgements

Many thanks to the magazines that first published some of these poems. "Free Ajami!" appeared in *Big Scream:* 55 (Fall 2016); "War" appeared in *Otoliths* (November, 2015). War was also translated to Italian by Angela D'Ambra and published in *YAWP*, 2020; Angela D'Ambra translated "The Trumpeters" for *Inverso* magazine, 2020, and *Inkroci* magazine, 2021; "The Trumpeters" translated by Yuliyana Todorova into Bulgarian published in the online magazine *Liternet.bg* in Sept 2019. "The Trumpeters" translated to Bulgarian by Yuliyana Todorova for *Liternet.bg,* translated to Spanish by Marco Vidal in *Alameda 39* issue #6, 2020 (Spain), and translated into Italian by Angela D'Ambra for publication in *Inkroci.* "The Trumpeters" also appeared in *Oakland Review, 100 Days Action,* and the anthology, *America, Poems for The Resistance!* (Spuyten Duyvil, 2017). "Terroristic" appeared in *LiVE MAG!* (2015) and appeared in *Wake Up and Dream* (MadHat Press, 2017). "Welcome to Sonoma County"/ "Benvenuto Nella Contea di Sonoma" was first published as an Italian/English chapbook published by Camion Editions (Torino, Italy 2019), and was then published in the anthology, *Good Cop/Bad Cop,* edited by Edward Vidaurre (FlowerSong Press, 2020). "Ode to the Deniers" appeared in *Open Your Eyes: an anthology on climate change* edited by Vinita Agrawal (Hawakal Publishers, Calcutta, West Bengal, India. 2020). "Warhawks" first appeared in *Madness Muse Press.* "Wrecking Crew After Parkland" appeared in *World Poetry Tree* e-book edited by Adel Khozam (UAE).

About the Author

Michael Rothenberg is co-founder of 100 Thousand Poets for Change, editor and publisher of BigBridge.org, and co-founder of Poets In Need, a non-profit 501(c)3, assisting poets in crisis. His most recent books of poetry include *Drawing The Shade* (Dos Madres Press), *Wake Up and Dream* (MadHat Press), and *In Memory of a Banyan Tree, Poems of the Outside World, 1985-2022* (Lost Horse Press). Recent translations include a bi-lingual edition of *Indefinite Detention: A Dog Story* (Varasek Ediciones, Madrid, Spain), and an Arabic edition of *Indefinite Detention: A Dog Story*, trans. by El Habib Louai, published in Cairo, Egypt by Arwiqa Publishers. Rothenberg lives in Tallahassee, Florida.

Author photo by Bob Howard

www.ingramcontent.com/pod-product-compliance
Lightning Source LLC
Chambersburg PA
CBHW011222120626
46545CB00010B/3117